INTRODUCING
LIBERATION
THEOLOGY

Leonardo Boff
Clodovis Boff

INTRODUCING
LIBERATION
THEOLOGY

Translated from the Portuguese by
Paul Burns

ORBIS BOOKS

Maryknoll, New York 10545

Seventeenth printing, October 2003

First published in this translation in Great Britain in 1987 by Burns & Oates/Search Press Ltd, Wellwood, North Farm Road, Tunbridge Wells, Kent TN2 3DR
Published in the United States of America by Orbis Books, Maryknoll, NY 10545

Published originally in Brazil in 1986 by Editora Vozes Ltda, Petrópolis, RJ, Brazil, under the title *Como fazer Teologia da Libertação*

Portuguese original © Leonardo Boff & Clodovis Boff 1986
This edition © Burns & Oates/Search Press Ltd 1987

Manuscript Editor: William E. Jerman

Library of Congress Cataloging-in-Publication Data

Boff, Leonardo.
  Introducing liberation theology.

    Translation of: Como fazer teologia da liberatção.
    Bibliography: p.
    1. Liberation theology.   I. Boff, Clodovis.
II. Title.
BT83.57.B59613   1987   230'.2   87-5672
ISBN 0-88344-575-1
ISBN 0-88344-550-6 (pbk.)

To:
Our friend Dom José Maria Pires,
archbishop of Paraíba,
theologian of a liberating pastoral practice
based on the poor and the blacks;

Our sister and companion Benedita Souza da Silva (Bené),
popular, ecumenical, and black theologian,
who took up the political diaconate
by taking the side of the workers;

Sergio Torres, liberation theologian and pastor,
builder of bridges in theological dialogue
on behalf of the poor of all continents.

Contents

Preface

Much has been written about liberation theology, but we felt there was still a need for a short book giving an overall, non-technical, and objective account of this new way of "doing theology."

This work is the fruit of an intense process of thinking and of commitment to the poor in order to bring about their liberation.

All that is said here is the responsibility of both authors without distinction, because it was conceived and worked out together, just as both of us, in fact, feel ourselves to be "brothers, sharing your sufferings, your kingdom, and all you endure" (Rev. 1:9).

Chapter 1

The Basic Question:
How to Be Christians
in a World of Destitution

A woman of forty, but who looked as old as seventy, went up to the priest after Mass and said sorrowfully: "Father, I went to communion without going to confession first." "How come, my daughter?" asked the priest. "Father," she replied, "I arrived rather late, after you had begun the offertory. For three days I have had only water and nothing to eat; I'm dying of hunger. When I saw you handing out the hosts, those little pieces of white bread, I went to communion just out of hunger for that little bit of bread." The priest's eyes filled with tears. He recalled the words of Jesus: "My flesh [bread] is real food . . . whoever feeds on me will draw life from me" (John 6:55, 57).

One day, in the arid region of northeastern Brazil, one of the most famine-stricken parts of the world, I (Clodovis) met a bishop going into his house; he was shaking. "Bishop, what's the matter?" I asked. He replied that he had just seen a terrible sight: in front of the cathedral was a woman with three small children and a baby clinging to her neck. He saw that they were fainting from hunger. The baby seemed to be dead. He said: "Give the baby some milk, woman!" "I can't, my lord," she answered. The bishop went on insisting that she should, and she that she could not. Finally, because of his insistence, she opened her blouse. Her breast was bleeding; the baby sucked violently at it. And sucked blood. The mother who had given it life was feeding it, like the pelican, with her own blood, her own life. The bishop knelt down in front of the woman, placed his hand on the baby's head, and there and then vowed that as long as such hunger existed, he would feed at least one hungry child each day.

One Saturday night I (Clodovis) went to see Manuel, a catechist of a base community. "Father," he said to me, "this community and others in the district are coming to an end. The people are dying of hunger. They are not coming: they haven't the strength to walk this far. They have to stay in their houses to save their energy. . . ."

Com-passion, "Suffering with"

What lies behind liberation theology? Its starting point is the perception of scandals such as those described above, which exist not only in Latin America but throughout the Third World. According to "conservative" estimates, there are in those countries held in underdevelopment:

- five-hundred million persons starving;
- one billion, six-hundred million persons whose life expectancy is less than sixty years (when a person in one of the developed countries reaches the age of forty-five, he or she is reaching middle age; in most of Africa or Latin America, a person has little hope of living to that age);
- one billion persons living in absolute poverty;
- one billion, five-hundred million persons with no access to the most basic medical care;
- five-hundred million with no work or only occasional work and a per capita income of less than $150 a year;
- eight-hundred-fourteen million who are illiterate;

• two billion with no regular, dependable water supply.

Who cannot be filled with righteous anger at such a human and social hell? Liberation theology presupposes an energetic protest at such a situation, for that situation means:

• on the social level: collective oppression, exclusion, and marginalization;

• on the individual level: injustice and denial of human rights;

• on the religious level: social sinfulness, "contrary to the plan of the Creator and to the honor that is due to him" (Puebla, §28).[1]

Without a minimum of "suffering with" this suffering that affects the great majority of the human race, liberation theology can neither exist nor be understood. Underlying liberation theology is a prophetic and comradely commitment to the life, cause, and struggle of these millions of debased and marginalized human beings, a commitment to ending this historical-social iniquity. The Vatican Instruction, "Some Aspects of Liberation Theology" (August 6, 1984), put it well: "It is not possible for a single instant to forget the situations of dramatic poverty from which the challenge set to theologians springs— the challenge to work out a genuine theology of liberation."

Meeting the Poor Christ in the Poor

Every true theology springs from a spirituality—that is, from a true meeting with God in history. Liberation theology was born when faith confronted the injustice done to the poor. By "poor" we do not really mean the poor individual who knocks on the door asking for alms. We mean a collective poor, the "popular classes," which is a much wider category than the "proletariat" singled out by Karl Marx (it is a mistake to identify the poor of liberation theology with the proletariat, though many of its critics do): the poor are also the workers exploited by the capitalist system; the underemployed, those pushed aside by the production process—a reserve army always at hand to take the place of the employed; they are the laborers of the countryside, and migrant workers with only seasonal work.

All this mass of the socially and historically oppressed makes up the poor as a social phenomenon. In the light of faith, Christians see in them the challenging face of the Suffering Servant, Jesus Christ. At first there is silence, silent and sorrowful contemplation, as if in the presence of a mystery that calls for introspection and prayer. Then this presence speaks. The Crucified in these crucified persons weeps and cries out: "I was hungry . . . in prison . . . naked" (Matt. 25:31–46).

Here what is needed is not so much contemplation as effective action for liberation. The Crucified needs to be raised to life. We are on the side of the poor only when we struggle alongside them against the poverty that has been unjustly created and forced on them. Service in solidarity with the oppressed also implies an act of love for the suffering Christ, a liturgy pleasing to God.

The First Step: Liberating Action, Liber-a(c)tion[2]

What is the action that will effectively enable the oppressed to move out of their inhuman situation? Many years of reflection and practice suggest that it has to go beyond two approaches that have already been tried: aid and reformism.

"Aid" is help offered by individuals moved by the spectacle of widespread destitution. They form agencies and organize projects: the "Band-Aid" or "corn-plaster" approach to social ills. But however perceptive they become and however well-intentioned—and successful—aid remains a strategy for helping the poor, but treating them as (collective) objects of charity, not as subjects of their own liberation. The poor are seen simply as those who have nothing. There is a failure to see that the poor are oppressed and made poor *by others;* and what they do possess—strength to resist, capacity to understand their rights, to organize themselves and transform a subhuman situation—tends to be left out of account. Aid increases the dependence of the poor, tying them to help from others, to decisions made by others: again, not enabling them to become their own liberators.

"Reformism" seeks to improve the situation of the poor, but always within existing social relationships and the basic structuring of society, which rules out greater participation by all and diminution in the privileges enjoyed by the ruling classes. Reformism can lead to great feats of development in the poorer nations, but this development is nearly always at the expense of the oppressed poor and very rarely in their favor. For example, in 1964 the Brazilian economy ranked 46th in the world; in 1984 it ranked 8th. The last twenty years have seen undeniable technological and industrial progress, but at the same time there has been a considerable worsening of social conditions for the poor, with exploitation, destitution, and hunger on a scale previously unknown in Brazilian history. This has been the price paid by the poor for this type of elitist, exploitative, and exclusivist development in which, in the words of Pope John Paul II, the rich become ever richer at the expense of the poor who become ever poorer.

The poor can break out of their situation of oppression only by working out a strategy better able to change social conditions: the strategy of liberation. In liberation, the oppressed come together, come to understand their situation through the process of conscientization,[3] discover the causes of their oppression, organize themselves into movements, and act in a coordinated fashion. First, they claim everything that the existing system can give: better wages, working conditions, health care, education, housing, and so forth; then they work toward the transformation of present society in the direction of a new society characterized by widespread participation, a better and more just balance among social classes and more worthy ways of life.

In Latin America, where liberation theology originated,

there have always been movements of liberation since the early days of the Spanish and Portuguese conquest. Amerindians, slaves, and the oppressed in general fought against the violence of the colonizers, created redoubts of freedom, such as the *quilombos* and *reducciones*,[4] led movements of revolt and independence. And among the colonizers were bishops such as Bartolomé de Las Casas, Antonio Valdivieso, and Toribio de Mogrovejo, and other missionaries and priests who defended the rights of the colonized peoples and made evangelization a process that included advancement of their rights.

Despite the massive and gospel-denying domination of the colonial centuries, dreams of freedom were never entirely extinguished. But it is only in the past few decades that a new consciousness of liberation has become widespread over the whole of Latin America. The poor, organized and conscientized, are beating at their masters' doors, demanding life, bread, liberty, and dignity. Courses of action are being taken with a view to release the liberty that is now held captive. Liberation is emerging as the strategy of the poor themselves, confident in themselves and in their instruments of struggle: free trade unions, peasant organizations, local associations, action groups and study groups, popular political parties, base Christian communities.[5] They are being joined by groups and individuals from other social classes who have opted to change society and join the poor in their struggle to bring about change.

The growth of regimes of "national security" (for which read "capital security"), of military dictatorships, with their repression of popular movements in many countries of Latin America, is a reaction against the transforming and liberating power of the organized poor.

The Second Step: Faith Reflects on Liberating Practice

Christians have always been and still are at the heart of these wider movements for liberation. The great majority of

Latin Americans are not only poor but also Christian. So the great question at the beginning and still valid today was—and is—what role Christianity has to play. How are we to be Christians in a world of destitution and injustice? There can be only one answer: we can be followers of Jesus and true Christians only by making common cause with the poor and working out the gospel of liberation. Trade union struggles, battles for land and for the territories belonging to Amerindians, the fight for human rights and all other forms of commitment always pose the same question: What part is Christianity playing in motivating and carrying on the process of liberating the oppressed?

Inspired by their faith—which must include commitment to one's neighbor, particularly to the poor, if it is to be true (Matt. 25:31–46)—and motivated by the proclamation of the kingdom of God—which begins in this world and culminates only in eternity—and by the life, deeds, and death of Christ, who made a historic option for the poor, and by the supremely liberating significance of his resurrection, many Christians— bishops, priests, religious, nuns, lay men and women—are throwing themselves into action alongside the poor, or joining the struggles already taking place. The Christian base communities, Bible societies, groups for popular evangelization, movements for the promotion and defense of human rights, particularly those of the poor, agencies involved in questions of land tenure, indigenous peoples, slums, marginalized groups, and the like, have all shown themselves to have more than a purely religious and ecclesial significance, and to be powerful factors for mobilization and dynamos of liberating action, particularly when they have joined forces with other popular movements.

Christianity can no longer be dismissed as the opium of the people, nor can it be seen as merely fostering an attitude of critique: it has now become an active commitment to liberation. Faith challenges human reason and the historical progress of the powerful, but in the Third World it tackles the problem of poverty, now seen as the result of oppression. Only from this starting point can the flag of liberation be raised.

The gospel is not aimed chiefly at "modern" men and women with their critical spirit, but first and foremost at "nonpersons," those whose basic dignity and rights are denied them. This leads to reflection in a spirit of prophecy and solidarity aimed at making nonpersons full human beings, and then new men and women, according to the design of the "new Adam," Jesus Christ.

Reflecting on the basis of practice, within the ambit of the vast efforts made by the poor and their allies, seeking inspiration in faith and the gospel for the commitment to fight against poverty and for the integral liberation of all persons and the whole person—that is what liberation theology means.

Christians who have been inspired by its principles and who live out its practices have chosen the harder way, exposing themselves to defamation, persecution, and even martyrdom. Many have been led by its insights and the practice of solidarity at its origins to a process of true conversion. Archbishop Oscar Romero of San Salvador, who had been conservative in his views, became a great advocate and defender of the poor when he stood over the dead body of Fr. Rutilio Grande, assassinated for his liberating commitment to the poor. The spilt blood of the martyr acted like a salve on his eyes, opening them to the urgency of the task of liberation. And he himself was to follow to a martyr's death in the same cause.

Commitment to the liberation of the millions of the oppressed of our world restores to the gospel the credibility it had at the beginning and at the great periods of holiness and prophetic witness in history. The God who pitied the downtrodden and the Christ who came to set prisoners free proclaim themselves with a new face and in a new image today. The eternal salvation they offer is mediated by the historical liberations that dignify the children of God and render credible the coming utopia of the kingdom of freedom, justice, love, and peace, the kingdom of God in the midst of human-kind.

From all this, it follows that if we are to understand the theology of liberation, we must first understand and take an active part in the real and historical process of liberating the oppressed. In this field, more than in others, it is vital to move beyond a merely intellectual approach that is content with comprehending a theology through its purely theoretical aspects, by reading articles, attending conferences, and skimming through books. We have to work our way into a more biblical framework of reference, where "knowing" implies loving, letting oneself become involved body and soul, communing wholly—being committed, in a word—as the prophet Jeremiah says: "He used to examine the cases of poor and needy, then all went well. Is not that what it means to know me?—it is Yahweh who speaks" (Jer. 22:16). So the criticisms made of liberation theology by those who judge it on a purely conceptual level, devoid of any real commitment to the oppressed, must be seen as radically irrelevant. Liberation theology responds to such criticism with just one question: What part have *you* played in the effective and integral liberation of the oppressed?

Notes

1. The Latin American bishops' conference, CELAM, has held three General Conferences since the Second Vatican Council. The second, held at Medellín, Colombia, in 1968, can be considered the "official launching" of the theme of liberation. The third, held at Puebla, Mexico, in 1979, with Pope John Paul II in attendance, developed in some ways, but also watered down, the conclusions reached at Medellín. Puebla produced its own "Final Document," published in England as *Puebla: Evangelization at Present and in the Future: Conclusions of the Third General Conference of the Latin American Bishops.* Catholic Institute for International Relations (Slough, Berkshire: St. Paul Publications, 1979) and in the U.S.A. as *Puebla and Beyond: Documentation and Commentary.*

Ed. John Eagleson and Philip Scharper (Maryknoll, N.Y.: Orbis, 1979).—TRANS.

2. The Portuguese word for "liberation" is *liberação,* which is composed of the root *liber,* "free," and, by chance, the Portuguese word for "action," *ação.* This coupling cannot be reproduced in English.—TRANS.

3. "Conscientization" was a term brought into general use by the Brazilian educator Paulo Freire. In his work with illiterate Brazilians, the basic learning unit was always linked with the social and political context of the learner, as distinguished from purely objective learning or indoctrination.—TRANS.

4. *Quilombos* were villages formed and inhabited by runaway slaves. *Reducciones* were enclaves of relative freedom from colonial powers for baptized Latin Americans, especially Amerindians, supervised by religious orders, especially the Jesuits, in Paraguay and elsewhere in the seventeenth and eighteenth centuries.—TRANS.

5. The Portuguese term *comunidade* (in Spanish, *comunidad) eclesial de base* is variously translated "base church community," "basic Christian community," "grass-roots community," etc. They are small groups that come together for Bible study, liturgy, and social action, usually without a priest but with trained leaders. Smaller than parishes, they represent the "base" of society. They are the operational base of liberation theology in practice.—TRANS.

Chapter 2

The Three Levels
of Liberation Theology:
Professional, Pastoral, Popular

From Head to Foot: A Continuum of Reflection

The term "liberation theology" conjures up the names of its best-known exponents such as Gustavo Gutiérrez, Jon Sobrino, and Pablo Richard. But liberation theology is a cultural and ecclesial phenomenon by no means restricted to a few professional theologians. It is a way of thinking that embraces most of the membership of the church, especially in the Third World.

In fact, at the "base" of the church there is a whole process of what one might call diffused and generalized theology of liberation going on in Christian base communities and Bible study groups. Their way of thinking is similar to that of the more nuanced theology of liberation pursued by professional theologians in that it also juxtaposes Christian faith and the situation of oppression. As we shall see, this is the basic constituent of liberation theology.

Between this basic level and the "highest," or professional, level of liberation theology, there is an intermediate level. This is the field of the thinking of bishops, priests, nuns, and other pastoral workers. This level serves as a sort of bridge between the thought of professional theologians and the liberating thought of the Christian "bases."

Each of these levels reflects the *same thing*: faith confronted with oppression. Each of them, however, reflects this faith *in its own way*—as we shall explain later. At this point it is important to note that from the bases to the highest level, going through the middle level, there is one continual flow of thought, one overall theological process at work.

Liberation theology could be compared to a tree. Those who see only professional theologians at work in it see only the branches of the tree. They fail to see the trunk, which is the thinking of priests and other pastoral ministers, let alone the roots beneath the soil that hold the whole tree—trunk and branches—in place. The roots are the practical living and thinking—though submerged and anonymous—going on in tens of thousands of base communities living out their faith and thinking it in a liberating key.

From this it will be seen that attacking the so-called liberation theologians merely lops off a few top branches. Liberation theology continues living in the trunk and still more so in the roots, hidden underground.

This also shows how this theological current is indissolubly linked to the very life of the people—to the faith and the struggle of the people. It has become part of their conception of the Christian life. It is also an organic part of the pastoral work carried out by priests and others, the theory behind their ministry. Once a theology has taken root as deeply as this, reached this level of incarnation in a people, once it has come to suffuse spirituality, liturgy, and ethics to this extent, and has become incarnated in social action, it has become virtually indestructible, as any analysis of religion will show.

The Levels of Liberation Theology

The table on page 13 shows in schematic form the three levels on which liberation is worked out, and how the three levels relate to each other.

The Three Levels of Liberation Theology

	Professional	*Pastoral*	*Popular*
Discourse	Detailed and rigorous	Organically related to practice	Diffuse and capillary, almost spontaneous
Logic	The logic of erudition: methodical, systematic, dynamic	The logic of action: specific, prophetic, propulsive	The logic of life: in words and deeds, sacramental
Method	Socio-analytical, hermeneutical, and theoretico-practical	Seeing, judging, acting	Confrontation: the gospel and life
Locus	Theological institutes, seminaries	Pastoral institutes, study centers	Bible study groups, base communities
Promoted through	Theological congresses	Pastoral congresses	Training courses
Practitioners	Theologians, professors, teachers	Pastoral ministers: priests, religious, lay persons	Members of base communities and their coordinators
Spoken works	Conference papers, lectures, seminar papers	Sermons, talks	Commentaries, celebrations, dramatizations
Written works	Books, articles	Pastoral instructions, guidelines	Notes, letters

This shows liberation theology to be a broad and variegated phenomenon. It encompasses a wide range of ways of thinking the faith in the face of oppression. Of course, when one speaks of liberation theology, one is generally using the term in reference to its expression in published form, and this is the sense in which it will most often be used in this book. But it is important not to lose sight of the rich and fruitful thinking at "base" level that feeds the professional work through which liberation theology has become known throughout the world.

What unites these three levels of theological-liberational thought? It is the one basic inspiration: a faith that transforms history, or, as others would put it, history seen from the basis of the ferment of faith. This means that the liberation theology of a Gustavo Gutiérrez is substantially the same as that of a Christian laborer in northeastern Brazil. The basic content is the same. The sap that feeds the branches of the tree is the same sap that passes through the trunk and rises from the hidden roots underground.

The distinction between the levels is in their logic, but more specifically in their language. Theology can be more or less articulate; popular theology will be expressed in everyday speech, with its spontaneity and feeling, whereas professional theology adopts a more scholarly language, with the structure and restraint proper to it.

It is not hard to see what liberation theology is when one starts at its roots—that is, by examining what the base communities do when they read the Bible and compare it with the oppression and longing for liberation in their own lives. But this is just what professional liberation theology is doing: it is simply doing it in a more sophisticated way. On the middle level, pastoral theology uses a language and approach that draw on both the ground level (concreteness, communicability, etc.) and the scholarly level (critical, systematic analysis and synthesis).

An Integrated and Integrating Theology

It is important to realize that these three sorts of theological reflection do not take place separately from or alongside each other. Most of the time they are practiced integrally, with integration at any level. So, for example, it can happen on the popular level with a pastor (priest or bishop) and a theologian sitting among the people, in the community center, reflecting on their struggle and their progress *with* them. Or it can take place at the professional level, when, for example, pastoral ministers and lay persons from base communities attend courses in systematic theology. There are more and more lay persons taking courses in theology or attending conferences on growth in faith.

But the most obvious integration is at the intermediate level, that of pastoral liberation theology. This is seen most clearly at church conferences, where you can find pastoral ministers—bishops, priests, religious, and lay persons—telling of their problems, Christians from base communities recounting their experiences, and theologians contributing their insights, deepening the meaning of the events under discussion and drawing conclusions from them. One notable aspect of these conferences is that they are not confined to church personnel: persons from other disciplines who can contribute and are committed to the progress of liberation also take part: sociologists, economists, teachers, technicians, all putting their professional expertise at the service of the people.

So one can see how liberation theology, at least the model of it that is emerging from a church committed to liberation, is a progressively integrating factor among pastors, theologians, and lay persons, all linked together around the same axis: their liberative mission. This is a long way from the old fragmentation, still largely operative, among a *canonical*, official theology, elaborated by curial and episcopal bodies, a *critical*, confrontational theology, elaborated in centers of study and research, and a *spontaneous* theology elaborated on the margins of the church.

All members of the people of God think about their faith: all of them, not only the professionals, "do" theology in a way. There can, indeed, be no faith without a minimum of theology. How so? Because faith is human and involves a "longing to understand"—*fides quaerens intellectum*—as the classic theologians put it. All who believe want to understand something of their faith. And as soon as you think about faith, you are already doing theology. So all Christians are in a certain sense theologians, and become more so the more they think about their faith. The subject of faith is the subject of theology—thinking and thought-out faith, cultivated collectively in the bosom of the church. The base communities, trying to draw lessons for today from the pages of the Gospels, are "doing" theology, theologizing. Furthermore, popular theology is thinking about the faith in solidarity: all give their opinions, completing or correcting those of others, each helping the other to assimilate the matter more clearly. Or is it that lay persons have no right to think? Are they just the "learning church," the taught church, and in no way the educating and educative church?

The Oral and Sacramental Character of Popular Liberation Theology

Popular theology is primarily oral; it is a spoken theology. Writing has a place in it as an aid to dialogue about faith, or as a reminder, a written collection of points that need to be recorded from what has been said before. But popular liberation theology is more than speech; it is a "sacramental" theology, expressed in gestures and symbols. For example, community members depict capitalism as a tree with rotten fruit and poison dripping from its branches. They bring gospel scenes to life though dramatic presentations. One gospel study group presented the situation of prostitutes today with a placard bearing the words, "Last in society, first in the kingdom." Another group, during a course on the Apocalypse, prepared their morning prayer by devising a silhouette show of a dragon with seven heads confronting a wounded lamb. They invited those present to give names to the dragon's seven heads. Men and women came forward and wrote, as best they could: "multinationals," "Law of National Security," "foreign debt," "military dictatorship," and names of various government officials held to be against the people. And below the lamb someone wrote: "Jesus Christ, Liberator." And a woman came forward and added: "The people of the poor."

There is genuine religious thinking behind this, a whole theology coming to light. Of course it is not called theology. Nor does it need to be. There is just the simple fact of an anonymous and collective theology with its own strength and truth. It is a theology in fact, just as folk remedies are real remedies.

Is it a critical theology? Yes, it is critical because it is clear and prophetic; critical, not in the academic sense, but really so because it gives an account of causes and puts forward measures for dealing with them. Often, it must be said, this means going way beyond the critical pretensions of the "doctors of theology" who can count every hair in the beast's coat but never look it in the face.

Pastoral Liberation Theology

There is such a thing as pastoral theology: it is the theology that sheds the light of the saving word on the reality of injustice so as to inspire the church to struggle for liberation. It is a theology in its own right: it follows the same basic lines as liberation theology as it is generally known. They both share the same root: evangelical faith; they both have the same objective: the liberating practice of love.

These two levels of theology are mutually enriching: theologians take up pastoral concepts and deepen them; pastors incorporate the most fruitful approaches and conclusions of professional theologians.

Pastors know how much they owe to the judgment of theologians. When Cardinal Joseph Ratzinger issued his "Instruction" on liberation theology, the bishops of Brazil, meeting in general assembly in April 1985, declared that, despite its possible "ambiguities and confusions," liberation theology "favors evangelization" in that it "clarifies the connection between movements seeking human liberation and the reality of the kingdom of God."

Bishops, like priests and other pastoral ministers, have not been content simply to take account of the liberation theology of the professional theologians. They have been doing their own liberation theology in accordance with their particular mission. What professional liberation theology enables them to do is to enrich their own reflections with its specific insights.

It is also worth pointing out that the institutional church has never considered any particular academic theology binding in faith—nor could it. The good news of the scriptures and the normative tradition of the church are enough for faith. But in order best to carry out their mission at each period of history, pastors—inevitably—turn to the theological currents that serve them best. This is what is happening now between pastors vowed to liberation of their people and theologians of liberation.

This is why there is a great spiritual harmony between professional and pastoral liberation theology in the church in the Third World. This can be seen with particular clarity in those bishops who devote their efforts to liberation. When the Brazilian bishops met for their general assembly on May 1, 1984, John Paul II gave them this provocative exhortation: "The bishops of Brazil are aware that they must liberate the people from injustices, which, I know, are grave. Let them take up their role as liberators of the people along the right way and using the right methods."

Well, a liberating bishop can adopt only a liberating pastoral theology.

How Liberation Theology Works in Practice

Liberation theology does not end with the production of theological works in centers of theological study and research, or institutions in which the church trains its priests and lay specialists. Such places are hardly the epicenters from which liberation theology emanates; its theologians are not armchair intellectuals, but rather "organic intellectuals" (in organic communion with the people) and "militant theologians," working with the pilgrim people of God and engaged in their pastoral responsibilities. They certainly keep one foot in centers of study, but their other foot is in the community.

Where is liberation theology to be found? You will find it at the base. It is linked with a specific community and forms a vital part of it. Its service is one of theological enlightenment of the community on its pilgrim way. You can find it any weekend in any slum, shantytown, or rural parish. It is there alongside the people, speaking, listening, asking questions, and being asked questions. It will not take shape in the form of an "ivory tower" theologian, one who is only a theologian and knows only theology. Liberation theology has to be skilled in the art of articulation to a high degree: it has to articulate the discourse of society, of the oppressed, of the world of popular, symbolic, and sacramental signs, with the discourse of faith and the normative tradition of the church. In the field of liberation, trying to know theology alone means condemning oneself to knowing not even one's own theology. So liberation theologians have to be at times pastors, analysts, interpreters, advocates, brothers or sisters in faith, and fellow pilgrims. Above all else, they have to be vehicles of the Spirit so as to be able to inspire and translate the demands of the gospel when confronted with the signs of the times as they are emerging among the poorer classes of society, in faithful reflection, hope, and committed love.

You will also find liberation theologians where the people of God congregates: in retreats, in diocesan planning meetings, in Bible study groups, in discussions of rural pastoral problems or discrimination against women, in debates on the problems of ethnic minority groups and cultures. In such groups their role is that of advisor. They hear the problems brought by the people, listen to the theology being done by and in the community—that is, the basic reflection that is the theology *of the people* reflecting on its life and progress. When invited to do so by the group, liberation theologians will then, from other points of view, try to ponder, deepen, and criticize the questions raised, always relating them to the word of revelation, the magisterium, and the normative tradition of the church.

Again, liberation theologians will be found in interdisciplinary discussion groups, round-table groups concerned with questions of social communications and the like, putting forward the view of a church that has taken seriously the option of solidarity with the poor. In all this, they will be doing theology *with* the people.

Finally, of course, liberation theologians will also be found at their desks, reading, researching, preparing their lectures and courses, writing books and articles. This is where they exercise the theoretical, professional side of their calling. This is where the experiences gathered at the base and the work done by pastoral ministers are critically examined, reflected on in depth, and worked into concepts—that is, dealt with according to the scientific criteria of theology. From here, theologians go out not only to do pastoral work and take part in meetings and discussions, but also to give lectures, to attend theological congresses, sometimes overseas, to speak in the centers of power and productivity. In this they are doing theology *from* the people.

Given the immense agenda of activities and all the practical and theoretical demands made on those who do this form of theology, it is not surprising that liberation theologians often experience fatigue, if tired, not exhaustion. Some questions go beyond an individual's capacity for reflection and exposition. This is why liberation theology is basically a task to be undertaken collectively, working in integral collaboration with the whole church, through the various kinds of activity already described.

When all is said and done, liberation theologians can claim no more than what Jesus taught his apostles: "We are merely servants; we have done no more than our duty" (Luke 17:10).

Chapter 3

How Liberation Theology Is Done

This chapter brings us to the kernel of this work. It is an attempt to explain the question of method; in other words, how liberation theology is "done."

The Preliminary Stage: Living Commitment

Before we can do theology we have to "do" liberation. The first step for liberation theology is pre-theological. It is a matter of trying to live the commitment of faith: in our case, to participate in some way in the process of liberation, to be committed to the oppressed.

Without this specific precondition, liberation theology would be simply a matter of words. So it is not enough here only to reflect on what is being practiced. Rather we need to establish a living link with living practice. If we fail to do this, then "poverty," "oppression," "revolution," "new society" are simply words that can be found in a dictionary.

The essential point is this: links with specific practice are *at the root* of liberation theology. It operates within the great dialectic of theory (faith) and practice (love).

In fact, it is *only* this effective connection with liberating practice that can give theologians a "new spirit," a new style, or a new way of doing theology. Being a theologian is not a matter of skillfully using methods but of being imbued with the theological spirit. Rather than introducing a new theological method, liberation theology is a new way of being a theologian. Theology is always a second step; the first is the "faith that makes its power felt through love" (Gal. 5:6). Theology (not the theologian) comes afterward; liberating practice comes first.

So first we need to have direct knowledge of the reality of oppression/liberation through objective engagement in solidarity with the poor. This pre-theological stage really means conversion of life, and this involves a "class conversion," in the sense of leading to effective solidarity with the oppressed and their liberation.

Three Forms of Commitment to the Poor

Of course the most appropriate and specific way for theologians to commit themselves to the poor and oppressed is to produce good theology. But what we want to stress here is that this is impossible without at least *some* contact with the world of the oppressed. Personal contact is necessary if one is to acquire new theological sensitivity.

Different forms and levels of contact can be taken up, depending on the inclinations and circumstances of persons interested:

• The first level might be called *more or less restricted,* either sporadic, in the form of visits to base communities, meetings, and the like, or more regular, through pastoral work on weekends, acting as advisor to communities or popular movements, and so forth.

• The second would be *alternating* periods of scholarly work—research, teaching, writing—with periods of practical work—pastoral or theological work in a particular church.

• The third level is that of those who live *permanently* with the people, making their home among the people, living and working alongside the people.

Whichever level is chosen, one point is paramount: anyone who wants to elaborate relevant liberation theology must be prepared to go into the "examination hall" of the poor. Only after sitting on the benches of the humble will he or she be entitled to enter a school of "higher learning."

Three Mediations

The elaboration of liberation theology can be divided into three basic stages, which correspond to the three traditional stages involved in pastoral work: seeing, judging, acting.

In liberation theology, we speak of three main "mediations": socio-analytical mediation, hermeneutical mediation, and practical mediation. The term "mediation" is used because the three stages represent means or instruments of the theological process. Briefly, these three mediations work and relate to each other as follows:

• Socio-analytical (or historico-analytical) mediation operates in the sphere of the world of the oppressed. It tries to find out why the oppressed are oppressed.

• Hermeneutical mediation operates in the sphere of God's world. It tries to discern what God's plan is for the poor.

• Practical mediation operates in the sphere of action. It tries to discover the courses of action that need to be followed so as to overcome oppression in accordance with God's plan.

Let us treat each of these mediations in more detail.

Socio-analytical Mediation

"Liberation" means liberation from oppression. Therefore, liberation theology has to begin by informing itself about the actual conditions in which the oppressed live, the various forms of oppression they may suffer.

Obviously, the prime object of theology is God. Nevertheless, before asking what oppression means in God's eyes, theologians have to ask more basic questions about the nature of actual oppression and its causes. The fact is that understanding God is not a substitute for or alternative to knowledge of the real world. As Thomas Aquinas said: "An error about the world redounds in error about God" (*Summa contra Gentiles,* II, 3).

Furthermore, if faith is to be efficacious, in the same way as Christian love, it must have its eyes open to the historical reality on which it seeks to work.

Therefore, to know the real world of the oppressed is a (material) part of the overall theological process. Though not the whole process in itself, it is an indispensable stage or mediation in the development of further and deeper understanding, the knowledge of faith itself.

Explaining the Phenomenon of Oppression

Faced with the oppressed, the theologian's first question can only be: Why is there oppression and what are its causes?

The oppressed are to be found in many strata of society. Puebla lists them: young children, juveniles, indigenous peoples, campesinos, laborers, the underemployed and unemployed, the marginalized, persons living in overcrowded urban slums, the elderly . . . (§§32–39). There is one overarching characteristic of the oppressed in the Third World: they are *poor* in socio-economic terms. They are the dispossessed masses on the peripheries of cities and in rural areas.

We need to start from here, from this "infrastructural" oppression, if we want to understand correctly all other forms of oppression and see how they relate to each other. In effect, as we shall see in more detail later, this socio-economic form conditions all other forms.

So, if we start with the fundamental expression of oppression as socio-economic poverty, we then need to find what causes it. Here, liberation theology has found three ready-made answers, which might be called the empirical, the functional, and the dialectical explanations of poverty.

The *empirical* explanation: poverty as vice. This approach produces a short and superficial explanation. It attributes the causes of poverty to laziness, ignorance, or simply human wickedness. It does not look at the collective or structural dimension of the problem: that the poor make up whole masses of a people and their numbers are growing all the time. It is the common conception of social destitution, the explanation most generally upheld in society.

From this viewpoint, the logical solution to the question of poverty is *aid*—in all its forms, from almsgiving on an individual basis to worldwide schemes. The poor are treated as objects of pity.

The *functional* explanation: poverty as backwardness. This is the liberal or bourgeois interpretation of the phenomenon of social poverty: it is attributed to economic and social backwardness. In time, thanks to the development process itself, helped in the Third World by foreign loans and technology, "progress" will arrive and hunger will disappear—so the functionalists think.

The social and political solution put forward here is *reform,* understood as the progressive betterment of the existing system. The poor are treated as passive objects of action taken by others.

The positive side of this approach is that it sees poverty as a *collective* phenomenon; it fails, however, to see it as *conflictive.* In other words, it fails to see what Puebla saw, that poverty "is not a passing phase. . . . It is the product of economic, social, and political situations and structures . . . where the rich get richer at the expense of the poor, who get even poorer" (§30).

The *dialectical* explanation: poverty as oppression. This sees poverty as the product of the economic organization of society itself, which *exploits* some—the workers—and *excludes* others from the production process—the underemployed, unemployed, and all those marginalized in one way or another. In his encyclical *Laborem Exercens* (chap. 3), Pope

John Paul II defines the root of this situation as the supremacy of capital—enjoyed by the few—over labor—practiced by the many.

This explanation, also called the "historico-structural" approach, sees poverty as a *collective* and also *conflictive* phenomenon, which can be overcome only by replacing the present social system with an *alternative* system. The way out of this situation is *revolution,* understood as the transformation of the bases of the economic and social system. Here the poor stand up as "subjects."

Historical Mediation and the Struggles of the Oppressed

The socio-analytical interpretation, as presented above, leads on to a historical approach to the problem of poverty. This approach focuses on the poor not only in their present situation, but as the end-product of a long process of plunder and social marginalization. It includes a consideration of the struggles of "the lowly" throughout their historical journey.

This shows that the situation of the oppressed is defined not only by their oppressors but also by the way in which they react to oppression, resist it, and fight to set themselves free from it. The poor cannot be understood without including their dimension as social subjects or co-agents—though submerged ones—of the historical process. This means that any analysis of the world of the poor has to take account not only of their oppressors but also of their own history and efforts at liberation, however embryonic these may be.

Relationships with Marxism

When dealing with the poor and the oppressed and seeking their liberation, how do we avoid coming into contact with Marxist groups (on the practical level) and with Marxist theory (on the academic level)? This is already hinted at in the use of such terms as "dialectical" or "historico-structural" explanation of the phenomenon of socio-economic poverty.

In liberation theology, Marxism is never treated as a subject on its own but always *from and in relation to the poor.* Placing themselves firmly on the side of the poor, liberation theologians ask Marx: "What can you tell us about the situation of poverty and ways of overcoming it?" Here Marxists are submitted to the judgment of the poor and their cause, and not the other way around.

Therefore, liberation theology uses Marxism purely as an *instrument.* It does not venerate it as it venerates the gospel. And it feels no obligation to account to social scientists for any use it may make—correct or otherwise—of Marxist terminology and ideas, though it does feel obliged to account to the poor, to their faith and hope, and to the ecclesial community, for such use. To put it in more specific terms, liberation theology freely borrows from Marxism certain "methodological pointers" that have proved fruitful in understanding the world of the oppressed, such as:

• the importance of economic factors;

• attention to the class struggle;

• the mystifying power of ideologies, including religious ones.

This is what the then superior general of the Jesuits, Fr. Pedro Arrupe, wrote in his well-known letter on Marxist analysis of December 8, 1980.

Liberation theology, therefore, maintains a decidedly critical stance in relation to Marxism. Marx (like any other Marxist) can be a companion on the way (see Puebla, §544), but he can never be *the* guide, because "You have only one teacher, the Christ" (Matt. 23:10). This being so, Marxist materialism and atheism do not even constitute a temptation for liberation theologians.

Enlarging on the Concept of "the Poor"

The Poor as Blacks, Indigenous Peoples, Women

Liberation theology is about liberation of the oppressed—in their totality as persons, body and soul—and in their totality as a class: the poor, the subjected, the discriminated against. We cannot confine ourselves to the purely socio-economic aspect of oppression, the "poverty" aspect, however basic and "determinant" this may be. We have to look also to other levels of social oppression, such as:

• racist oppression: discrimination against blacks;

• ethnic oppression: discrimination against indigenous peoples or other minority groups;

• sexual oppression: discrimination against women.

Each of these various oppressions—or discriminations—and more (oppression of children, juveniles, the elderly) has its specific nature and therefore needs to be treated (in both theory and practice) specifically. So we have to go beyond an exclusively "classist" concept of the oppressed, which would restrict the oppressed to the socio-economically poor. The ranks of the oppressed are filled with others besides the poor.

Nevertheless, we have to observe here that the socio-economically oppressed (the poor) do not simply exist *along-side* other oppressed groups, such as blacks, indigenous peoples, women—to take the three major categories in the Third World. No, the "class-oppressed"—the socio-economically poor—are the infrastructural expression of the process of oppression. The other groups represent "super-structural" expressions of oppression and because of this are deeply conditioned by the infrastructural. It is one thing to be a black taxi-driver, quite another to be a black football idol; it is one thing to be a woman working as a domestic servant, quite another to be the first lady of the land; it is one thing to be an Amerindian thrown off your land, quite another to be an Amerindian owning your own farm.

This shows why, in a class-divided society, class struggles—which are a fact and an ethical demonstration of the presence of the injustice condemned by God and the church—are the main sort of struggle. They bring antagonistic groups, whose basic interests are irreconcilable, face to face. On the other hand, the struggles of blacks, indigenes, and women bring groups that are not naturally antagonistic into play, whose basic interests can in principle be reconciled. Although exploiting bosses and exploited workers can never finally be reconciled (so long as the former remain exploiters and the latter exploited), blacks can be reconciled with whites, indigenes with nonindigenes, and women with men. We are dealing here with nonantagonistic contradictions mixed in with the basic, antagonist class conflict in our societies. But it must also be noted that noneconomic types of oppression aggravate preexisting socio-economic oppression. The poor are additionally oppressed when, beside being poor, they are also black, indigenous, women, or old.

The Poor as "Degraded and Deprived"

The socio-analytical approach is undoubtedly important for a critical understanding of the situation of the poor and all classes of oppressed. Nevertheless, its insight into oppression is limited to what an academic sort of approach can achieve. Such an approach has its limitations, which are those of analytical scholarship. It can only (but this is already a great deal) grasp the basic and overall structure of oppression; it leaves out of account all the shadings that only direct experience and day-by-day living can appreciate. Attending just to the rational, scientific understanding of oppression falls into rationalism and leaves more than half the reality of the oppressed poor out of account.

The oppressed are more than what social analysts— economists, sociologists, anthropologists—can tell us about them. We need to listen to the oppressed themselves. The poor, in their popular wisdom, in fact "know" much more about poverty than does any economist. Or rather, they know in another way, in much greater depth.

For example, what is "work" for popular wisdom and what is it for an economist? For the latter it is usually a simple category or a statistical calculation, whereas for the people, "work" means drama, anguish, dignity, security, exploitation, exhaustion, life—a whole series of complex and even contradictory perceptions. Again, what does "land" mean to an agricultural worker and what does it mean to a sociologist? For the former, it is much more than an economic and social entity; it is human greatness, with a deeply affective and even mystical significance. And if it is your ancestral land, then it means even more.

Finally, "poor" for the people means dependence, debt, exposure, anonymity, contempt, and humiliation. The poor do not usually refer to themselves as "poor," which would offend their sense of honor and dignity. It is the non-poor who call them poor. So a poor woman from Tacaimbó in the interior of Pernambuco, hearing someone call her poor, retorted: "Poor, no! Poor is the end. We are the dispossessed, but fighting!"

From which we conclude that liberation theologians in contact with the people cannot be content with social analyses but also have to grasp the whole rich interpretation made by the poor of their world, linking the socio-analytical approach with the indispensable understanding provided by folk wisdom.

The Poor as the Disfigured Son of God

Finally, the Christian view of the poor is that they are all this and more. Faith shows us the poor and all the oppressed in the light that liberation theology seeks to project (and here we anticipate the hermeneutical mediation):

- the disfigured image of God;
- the Son of God made the suffering servant and rejected;
- the memorial of the poor and persecuted Nazarene;
- the sacrament of the Lord and Judge of history.

Without losing any of its specific substance, the conception of the poor is thus infinitely enlarged through being opened up to the Infinite. In this way, seen from the standpoint of faith and the mission of the church, the poor are not merely human beings with needs; they are not just persons who are socially oppressed and at the same time agents of history. They are all these and more: they are also bearers of an "evangelizing potential" (Puebla, §1147) and beings called to eternal life.

Hermeneutical Mediation

Once they have understood the real situation of the oppressed, theologians have to ask: What has the word of God to say about this? This is the second stage in the theological construct—a specific stage, in which discourse is *formally* theological.

It is therefore a question, at this point, of seeing the "oppression/liberation" process "in the light of faith." What does this mean? The expression does not denote something vague or general; it is something that has a positive meaning in scripture, where we find that "in the light of faith" and "in the light of the word of God" have the same meaning.

The liberation theologian goes to the scriptures bearing the whole weight of the problems, sorrows, and hopes of the poor, seeking light and inspiration from the divine word. This is a new way of reading the Bible: the hermeneutics of liberation.

The Bible of the Poor

An examination of the whole of scripture from the viewpoint of the oppressed: this is the hermeneutics or specific interpretation (reading) used by liberation theology.

We must say straightaway that this is not the only possible and legitimate reading of the Bible. For us in the Third World today, however, it is the obvious one, the "hermeneutics for our times." From the heart of the great revelation in the Bible, it draws the most enlightening and eloquent themes that speak to the poor: God the father of life and advocate of the oppressed, liberation from the house of bondage, the prophecy of a new world, the kingdom given to the poor, the church as total sharing. The hermeneutics of liberation stresses these veins, but not to the exclusion of everything else. They may not be the most *important* themes in the Bible (in themselves), but they are the most *relevant* (to the poor in their situation of oppression). But then it is the order of importance that determines the order of relevance.

Furthermore, the poor are not simply poor, as we have seen; they seek life, and "to the full" (John 10:10). This means that questions relevant to or urgent for the poor are bound up with the transcendental questions of conversion, grace, resurrection.

In effect, the hermeneutics of liberation questions the word of God without anticipating the divine response. Because it is a theological exercise, this hermeneutics is done in fidelity— that is, in openness to God's ever new and always surprising revelation—to the foundational message that can save or condemn. This means that the response of the word can always call the question itself into question, or even the questioners, to the extent that it calls them to conversion, faith, and commitment to justice.

There is, nevertheless, a "hermeneutical circle" or "mutual appeal" between the poor and the word (Paul VI, *Evangelii nuntiandi,* no. 29). But there is no denying that the lead in this dialectic belongs to the sovereign word of God, which must retain primacy of value, though not necessarily of methodology. On the other hand, we know from the intrinsically liberating content of biblical revelation that for the poor the word can emerge only as a message of radical consolation and liberation.

The Marks of a Theological-liberative Hermeneutics

The rereading of the Bible done from the basis of the poor and their liberation project has certain characteristic marks.

It is a hermeneutics that favors *application* rather than explanation. In this the theology of liberation takes up the kind of probing that has been the perennial pursuit of all true biblical reading, as can be seen, for example, in the church fathers—a pursuit that was neglected for a long time in favor of a rationalistic exegesis concerned with dragging out the meaning-in-itself.

Liberative hermeneutics reads the Bible as a book of life, not as a book of strange stories. The textual meaning is indeed sought, but only as a function of the *practical* meaning: the important thing is not so much interpreting the text of the scriptures as interpreting life "according to the scriptures." Ultimately, this old/new reading aims to find contemporary actualization (practicality) for the textual meaning.

Liberative hermeneutics seeks to discover and activate the *transforming energy* of biblical texts. In the end, this is a question of finding an interpretation that will lead to individual change (conversion) and change in history (revolution). This is not a reading from ideological preconceptions: biblical religion is an open and dynamic religion thanks to its messianic and eschatological character. Ernst Bloch once declared: "It would be difficult to make a revolution without the Bible."

Finally, without being reductionist, this theological-political rereading of the Bible stresses the *social context* of the message. It places each text in its historical context in order to construct an appropriate—not literal—translation into our own historical context. For example, liberative hermeneutics will stress (but not to the exclusion of other aspects) the social context of oppression in which Jesus lived and the markedly political context of his death on the cross. Obviously, when it is approached in this way, the biblical text takes on particular relevance in the context of the oppression now being experienced in the Third World, where liberating evangelization has immediate and serious political implications—as the growing list of martyrs in Latin America proves.

Biblical Books Favored by Liberation Theology

Theology must, of course, take all the books of the Bible into account. Nevertheless, hermeneutical preferences are inevitable and even necessary, as the liturgy and the practice of homiletics demonstrate. The books most appreciated by liberation theology, on its three levels—professional, pastoral, and especially popular—are:

• *Exodus,* because it recounts the epic of the politico-religious liberation of a mass of slaves who, through the power of the covenant with God, became the people of God;

• the *Prophets,* for their uncompromising defense of the liberator God, their vigorous denunciation of injustices, their revindication of the rights of the poor, and their proclamation of the messianic world;

• the *Gospels,* obviously, for the centrality of the divine person of Jesus, with his announcement of the kingdom, his liberating actions, and his death and resurrection—the final meaning of history;

• the *Acts of the Apostles,* because they portray the ideal of a free and liberating Christian community;

• *Revelation,* because in collective and symbolic terms it describes the immense struggles of the people of God against all the monsters of history.

In some places, other books too are favored, such as the *Wisdom* books, because they embody the value of divine revelation contained in popular wisdom (proverbs, legends, etc.). In some parts of Central America, after the base communities had meditated on the books of the *Maccabees* to inspire their faith in the context of armed uprising (legitimized, it may be noted, by their pastors), once the war was over and the period of national reconstruction began, Christians turned to a systematic reading of the books of *Ezra* and *Nehemiah,* which portray the efforts at restoring the people of God after the critical period in Babylonian captivity.

We hardly need to say here that any book of the Bible has to be read in a christological key—that is, based on the high point of revelation as found in the Gospels. The viewpoint of the poor is thus placed within a wider viewpoint—that of the lord of history—whence the word of God derives its consistency and strength.

Recovering the Great Christian Tradition
in the Perspective of Liberation

Liberation theology is conscious of being a new theology, linked with the current period of history and addressed to the great masses, both Christian and non-Christian, in the Third World. Nonetheless, it sees itself as maintaining a basic link of continuity with the living tradition of the faith of the Christian church. It looks to the past in an effort to learn from it and enrich itself. With regard to theological tradition, it maintains a twofold stance.

With respect to the limits and incompleteness of the systems of the past—at least in part an inevitable consequence of their historical setting—liberation theology maintains a stance of *criticism.* For example, the Scholastic theology of the eleventh to the fourteenth century made undeniable contributions to the precise and systematic presentation of Christian truth, but liberation theology criticizes it for its overbearing tendency to theoreticism, to voiding the world of its historical character (a *static* vision of things), showing precious little sensitivity to the social question of the poor or their historical liberation. As for classic spirituality, liberation theology seeks to correct its ahistorical interiority, its elitism, and its deficient sense of the presence of the lord of history in liberative social processes.

With respect to incorporating overlooked but fruitful theological strains that can enrich and challenge us today, liberation theology maintains a stance of *retrieval.* Thus, from the patristic theology of the second to the ninth century, we can reincorporate its deeply unitary sense of the history of salvation, its feeling for the social demands of the gospel, its perception of the prophetic dimension of the mission of the church, its sensitivity to the poor.

Liberation theology also finds inspiration in the individual evangelical experiences of so many saints and prophets, many of them declared heretics at the time, but whose liberating impact can clearly be seen today—Francis of Assisi, Savonarola, Meister Eckhart, Catherine of Siena, Bartolomé de Las Casas, and, from recent times, Frs. Hidalgo, Morelos, Cícero. Nor should we forget the valuable contribution of the "common life" and other similar reform movements of the Middle Ages, or the evangelical postulates of the great Reformers.

Liberation Theology and the Social Teaching of the Church

Liberation theology also has an open and positive relationship with the social teaching of the church. We have to say at once that liberation theology does not set out to be in *competition* with the teaching of the magisterium. Nor could it, because the two sets of discourse operate on different levels and have differing objectives. But to the extent that the social teaching of the church provides broad guidelines for Christian social activity, liberation theology tries, on the one hand, to *integrate* these guidelines into its own synthesis, and, on the other, to *clarify* them in a creative manner for the specific context of the Third World.

This work of integration and clarification is founded in the dynamic and open nature of the social teachings of the church (see Puebla, §§473 and 539). Furthermore, by this work, liberation theology is paying heed to the explicit appeal of the magisterium itself, which, through Paul VI's *Octogesima Adveniens,* stated:

It is not our ambition, nor even our mission . . . to pronounce one word for all or to put forward one universal solution. It is for the Christian communities to analyze, objectively, the situation in their own countries; try to shed light on it with the light of the unalterable words of the gospel; discern the *options and commitments* which they need to take in order to bring about social changes [no. 4; see also nos. 42 and 48].

This is a precise indication of the three stages of theological-liberative investigation by which what is less specific in the teaching of the church can become more specific.

Paul VI launched a challenge to the social teaching of the church when he said it was "not limited to recalling a few general principles, but is, on the contrary, something that develops through means of a reflection carried on in permanent contact with the situations of this world" (ibid., no. 42). By taking up this challenge, liberation theology places itself fully in line with the requirements of the teaching of the church. This is also taken into account when it is worked out by pastors in the form of liberation theology on the pastoral level.

Furthermore, Cardinal Ratzinger himself, in his instruction on liberation theology (chap. 5), considers the social teaching of the church as a sort of preliberation theology, or "pastoral theology of liberation," insofar as it tries to "respond to the challenge posed to our time by oppression and hunger" (no. 1).

The only conclusion one can draw from all this is that there is *no* incompatibility of principle between the social teaching of the church and liberation theology. One complements the other for the good of the whole people of God.

The Creative Task of Theology

Armed with its own techniques and all the material it has thereby accumulated, liberation theology sets out to build up truly new syntheses of faith and to put together theoretically new answers to the great challenges of the times. It is not just an accumulator of theological material, but a true architect. So it arms itself with the necessary theoretical daring and with a good dose of creative imagination in order to tackle previously unknown questions posed today by the continents under oppression.

By creatively bringing out or deducing the liberating content of faith, liberation theology seeks to produce a new codification of the Christian mystery, thereby helping the church to carry out its mission of liberative evangelization in history.

Practical Mediation

Liberation theology is far from being an inconclusive theology. It starts from action and leads to action, a journey wholly impregnated by and bound up with the atmosphere of faith. From analysis of the reality of the oppressed, it passes through the word of God to arrive finally at specific action. "Back to action" is a characteristic call of this theology. It seeks to be a militant, committed, and liberating theology.

It is a theology that leads to practical results because today, in the world of the "wretched of the earth," the *true form* of faith is "political love" or "macro-charity." Among the poorest of the Third World, faith is not only "also" political, but *above all else* political.

But despite all this, faith cannot be reduced to action, however liberating it may be. It is "always greater" and must always include moments of contemplation and of profound thanksgiving. Liberation theology also leads one up to the Temple. And from the Temple it leads back once more to the practice of history, now equipped with all the divine and divinizing powers of the Mystery of the world.

And so, yes: liberation theology leads to action: action for justice, the work of love, conversion, renewal of the church, transformation of society.

Who Designs the Program of Action?

The logic of this third stage—practical mediation—has its own internal regimen. Naturally, the definition of action depends on the theological level on which one finds oneself: professional, pastoral, or popular.

A professional theologian can point only to broad lines of action. A pastor-theologian can be more definite as to courses of action to be followed. A popular theologian is in a position to be able to go deeply into the particular course to be followed in a specific case. But on both the last levels—pastoral and popular—the definition of action can of course be only a collective task, carried out by all those involved in the particular question of the moment.

The process of acting is extremely complex. It involves a number of steps, such as reasonable and prudent appreciation of all the circumstances, and attempting to foresee the consequences of the action planned. Whatever else it may involve, any course of action is likely to have to take the following elements into consideration:

• A decision as to what is *historically viable,* or at least possible, through analyzing one's own and the opposition's forces, without underestimating the resistance and opposition of those who want to preserve the status quo in society and in the church, and without being utopian or satisfied with "good intentions."

• Defining one's *strategy* and *tactics,* favoring nonviolent methods, such as dialogue, persuasion, moral pressure, passive resistance, evangelical resoluteness, and other courses of action sanctioned by the ethic of the gospel: marches, strikes, street demonstrations, and, as a last resort, recourse to physical force.

• Coordinating *micro-actions* with the *macro-system,* so as to give them—and ensure they retain—an effectively critical and transformative orientation.

• Articulating the action of the people of God with that of *other historical forces* present in society.

• Drawing up a *program* (blueprint) for action, inspiring and encouraging the people to struggle, the program being, as it were, the bridge between decision-making and implementation.

In this third stage, more knowledge is gained in practice than from theory. In other words, it is easier to experience than to think out. Therefore on this level, wisdom and prudence are more useful than is analytical reasoning. And in this, ordinary persons are often way ahead of the learned.

By Way of Example: How to Do a "Theology of Land"

Having come to the end of our exposition of the methodology of liberation theology, it seems appropriate to give an example of how the three stages work out in practice, each with its specific requirements. Let us take, for good reasons, the theme of "land." Depending on the degree of explicitation required at any of the three levels—professional, pastoral, and popular—this is how the steps in working out a "theology of land" might be summarized:

Step Zero: Participation
• being involved in the specific problem concerning land in the area, working in rural base communities, being active in trade unions, taking part in harvests and other field tasks, participating in the struggles of rural workers, and so forth.
Step one: Socio-analytical mediation (seeing)
• analyze the land situation as it affects the nation as a whole or the particular area where one is working;
• encourage rural workers to stand up for themselves;
• see how individuals experience their problems and how they resist oppression or organize their resistance to it.
Step two: Hermeneutical mediation (judging)
• evaluating how the populace faces up to the land question on the basis of its religion and faith;
• evaluating how the Bible views land (gift of God, promised land, symbol of the final kingdom to come, etc.);

• determining how theological tradition, especially as expressed by the church fathers, sees the question of land (common ownership, nonmercantile character of land, etc.).

Step three: Practical mediation (acting)

• stressing the value of worker unity and organization: unions, cooperatives, or other movements;

• publicizing the need for agrarian reform to be brought about by those who work the land;

• making a choice of particular banners under which to fight, linking with other forces, forecasting possible consequences, possible allocation of tasks, etc.

Chapter 4

Key Themes of Liberation Theology

We now need to see what overall conclusions liberation theology has reached by using the methodology set out in the preceding chapter. So let us describe briefly some of the key themes that make up the content of this way of thinking and acting in the light of faith. But first we must stress once more that we are not dealing with a new faith, but with the faith of the Apostles, the faith of the church linked to the sufferings and hopes for liberation of the oppressed of this world. So we need to ask: What liberating potential is contained in the Christian faith, a faith that promises eternal life but also a worthy and just life on this earth? What image of God emerges from the struggles of the oppressed for their liberation? What aspects of the mystery of Christ take on particular relevance? What accents do the poor give to their Marian devotion?

Let us begin by delineating the overall view a little more clearly—that is, by defining the perspective from which we have to approach all these subjects: the perspective of the poor and their liberation.

Solidarity with the Poor: Worshiping God and Communing with Christ

Liberation theology can be understood as the reflection in faith of the church that has taken to heart the "clear and prophetic option expressing preference for, and solidarity with, the poor" (Puebla, §1134). It is for them, and with them, that the church seeks to act in a liberative manner. Such an option is neither self-interested nor political, as would be the option of the institutional church for an emergent historical power—the popular classes taking an ever more dominant role in the conduct of affairs. No, this option is made for intrinsic reasons, for reasons inherent in the Christian faith itself. Let us look at them one by one.

Theological Reasons for the Option for the Poor

Theo-logical Motivation (on God's Part)

The biblical God is fundamentally a living God, the author and sustainer of all life. Whenever persons see their lives threatened, they can count on the presence and power of God who comes to their aid in one form or another. God feels impelled to come to the help of the oppressed poor: "I have seen the miserable state of my people in Egypt. I have heard their appeal to be free of their slave-drivers. Yes, I am well aware of their sufferings. . . . And now the cry of the sons of Israel has come to me, and I have witnessed the way in which the Egyptians oppress them" (Exod. 3:7, 9). The worship that is pleasing to God must be a "search for justice" and a turning to the needy and the oppressed (see Isa. 1:10–17; 58:6–7; Mark 7:6–13). By opting for the poor, the church imitates our Father who is in heaven (Matt. 5:48).

Christological Motivation (on Christ's Part)

Christ undeniably made a personal option for the poor and held them to be the main recipients of his message (see Luke 6:20; 7:21–22). They fulfill his law of love who, like the good Samaritan (Luke 10:25–37), approach those who have fallen by the wayside, who make into neighbors those who are distant from them, and make neighbors into brothers and sisters. The followers of Christ make this option for the poor and needy the first and foremost way of expressing their faith in Christ in the context of widespread poverty in the world of today.

Eschatological Motivation (from the Standpoint of the Last Judgment)

The gospel of Jesus is quite clear on this point: at the supreme moment of history, when our eternal salvation or damnation will be decided, what will count will be our attitude of acceptance or rejection of the poor (Matt. 25:31–46). The Supreme Judge stands by the side of anyone who is oppressed, seen as a sister or brother of Jesus: "I tell you solemnly, insofar as you did it to one of these least brothers of mine, you did it to me" (Matt. 25:40). Only those who commune in his history with the poor and needy, who are Christ's sacraments, will commune definitively with Christ.

Apostolic Motivation (on the Part of the Apostles)

From its earliest days the church showed concern for the poor. The Apostles and their followers held all things in common so that there would be no poor among them (see Acts 2 and 4). In proclaiming the gospel, the one thing they emphasized was that the poor should not be ignored: "The only thing they insisted on was that we should remember to help the poor, as indeed I was anxious to do" (Gal. 2:10). As the greatest of the Greek fathers, St. John Chrysostom, put it, for the sake of the mission of the church, humankind was divided into pagans and Jews, but with reference to the poor there was no division made whatsoever, because they all belonged to the common mission of the church, as much to that of Peter (to the Jews) as to that of Paul (to the pagans).

Ecclesiological Motivation (on the Part of the Church)

Faced with the marginalization and impoverishment of the great majority of its members, the church of Latin America, moved by the motivations listed above and seized with a humanistic sense of compassion, has made a solemn "preferential option for the poor," defined at the Medellín conference in 1968 and ratified at Puebla in 1979, when the bishops reaffirmed "the need for conversion on the part of the whole church to a preferential option for the poor, an option aimed at their integral liberation" (§1134).

Because of the sufferings and struggles of the poor, the church in its evangelization seeks to urge all Christians to live their faith in such a way that they also make it a factor for transforming society in the direction of greater justice and fellowship. All need to make the option for the poor: the rich with generosity and no regard for reward, the poor for their fellow poor and those who are even poorer than they.

In the Final Analysis, Who Are the Poor?

This question is often posed by those who cannot really be counted among the poor. They come up with so many definitions and subdivisions of poverty that any real meaning in the term is dissipated, and they end up seeing themselves as one sort of poor—usually the "poor in spirit." When those who are actually poor (lacking the means to sustain life) discuss the question, they easily come to an objective assessment of the situation and of specific remedies that would liberate them from their situation of dehumanizing poverty.

In the context of our examination of liberation theology, we can make a distinction between two basic classes of the poor.

The Socio-economically Poor

These are all those who lack or are deprived of the necessary means of subsistence—food, clothing, shelter, basic health care, elementary education, and work. There is such a thing as innocent poverty, independent of any will or system (infertile land, chronic drought, etc.), but today, in most cases, widespread poverty is maintained by the capitalist system that derives cheap labor from it; this prevents a region or people from being developed, excluding them from minimal human advancement.

There is also a socio-economic poverty that is unjust because it is produced by a process of exploitation of labor, as denounced by John Paul II in his encyclical *Laborem Exercens* (no. 8). Workers are not paid a just wage, the price of raw materials is held down, the interest charged on loans needed by cooperatives is exorbitant. Poverty in such cases means impoverishment and constitutes injustice on a societal and even international scale.

As we have said, there are various forms of poverty brought about by socio-economic circumstances, which in addition embody specific oppressions and therefore require specific forms of liberation. So there are those who are *discriminated* against by reason of their race (such as blacks), by reason of their culture (such as native tribes), or by reason of their sex (women). The poorest of the poor are often to be found among such groups, for they incur the whole gamut of oppressions and discriminations. In one base community a woman described herself as oppressed and impoverished on six counts: as a woman, as a prostitute, as a single parent, as black, as poor, and because of her tribal origin. Faced with such conditions, what can being a Christian mean except living the faith in a liberating way, trying every possible avenue of escape from such a set of social iniquities? We have to tell poor persons like her that God loves them in a special way, whatever moral or personal situation they find themselves in, because God in Jesus established solidarity with the poor, especially in his passion and death: "For this reason alone, the poor merit preferential attention, whatever may be the moral or personal situation in which they find themselves" (Puebla,

§1142). They are preferred by God and by Christ not because they are good, but because they are poor and wronged. God does not will the poverty they suffer.

Their situation of poverty constitutes a challenge to God himself in his innermost nature and to the Messiah in his mission to restore rights taken away, to bring justice to the helpless and comfort to the abandoned.

The Evangelically Poor

They are all those who place themselves and their strength at the service of God and their sisters and brothers; all those who do not put themselves first, who do not see their security and the meaning of their lives and actions in profiting from this world and accumulating possessions, honor, power, and glory, but open themselves to God in gratitude and disinterestedly serve others, even those they hate, building up means of producing a more worthy life for all. Faced with a predatory, consumerist society, the evangelically poor will use the goods of this world with moderation and sharing. They are neither rigid ascetics who disdain God's creation with all the good things God has placed at the disposal of all, nor spendthrifts who intemperately and selfishly take all they can for themselves. The evangelically poor are those who make themselves available to God in the realization of God's project in this world, and thereby make themselves into instruments and signs of the kingdom of God. The evangelically poor will establish solidarity with the economically poor and even identify with them, just as the historical Jesus did.

Those who, without being socio-economically poor, make themselves poor—out of love for and solidarity with the poor—in order to struggle against unjust poverty with them and together seek liberation and justice, are evangelically poor to a preeminent degree. They do not seek to idealize either material poverty, which they see as a consequence of the sin of exploitation, or riches, which they see as the expression of oppressive and selfish accumulation of goods; instead they seek the means to social justice for all. In the Third World context, one cannot be evangelically poor without being in solidarity with the lives, causes, and struggles of the poor and oppressed.

Sometimes love for the poor can become so intense that individuals give up their own station in life to share in the sufferings of the poor, even to the point of sharing their premature death. This is perfect liberation, for they have set themselves free from themselves and, in following Jesus, the poor man from Nazareth, they have freed themselves fully for others and for the God dwelling within these others.

Liberation theology would like to see all Christians, including the socio-economically poor, evangelically poor. It seeks, in the light of the challenges posed by the oppressed poor, to work out and apply the liberating dimension of faith so that the fruits of the kingdom of God can be enjoyed within history. These fruits are, principally, gratitude to the Father, acceptance of divine adoption, life and justice for all, and universal fellowship.

Let us now see how the classic themes of our faith can be seen in relation to liberation and the kingdom.

Some Key Themes of Liberation Theology

1. *Living and true faith includes the practice of liberation.* Faith is the original standpoint of all theology, including liberation theology. Through the act of faith we place our life, our pilgrimage through this world, and our death in God's hands. By the light of faith we see that divine reality penetrates every level of history and the world. As a way of life, faith enables us to discern the presence or negation of God in various human endeavors. It is living faith that provides a contemplative view of the world.

But faith also has to be true, the faith necessary for salvation. In the biblical tradition it is not enough for faith to be

true in the terms in which it is expressed (orthodoxy); it is veri-
fied, made true, when it is informed by love, solidarity, hunger
and thirst for justice. St. James teaches that "faith without
good deeds is useless" and that believing in the one God is not
enough, for "the demons have the same belief" (2:21, 20).
Therefore, ortho-doxy has to be accompanied by ortho-
praxis. Living and true faith enables us to hear the voice of the
eschatological Judge in the cry of the oppressed: "I was
hungry . . ." (Matt. 25:35). This same faith bids us give heed
to that voice, resounding through an act of liberation: "and
you gave me to eat." Without this liberating practice that
appeases hunger, faith barely plants a seed, let alone produces
fruit: not only would we be failing to love our sisters and
brothers but we would be failing to love God too: "If a man
who was rich enough in this world's goods saw that one of his
brothers was in need, but closed his heart to him, how could
the love of God be living in him?" (1 John 3:17). Only the faith
that leads on to love of God and love of others is the faith that
saves, and therefore promotes integral liberation: "Our love is
not to be just words and mere talk, but something real and
active" (1 John 3:18).

It is the task of liberation theology to recover the practical
dimension inherent in biblical faith: in the world of the oppressed this practice can only be liberating.

2. *The living God sides with the oppressed against the
pharaohs of this world.* In a world in which death from hunger
and repression have become commonplace, it is important to
bring out those characteristics of the Christian God that di-
rectly address the practice of liberation. God will always be
God and as such will constitute the basic mystery of our faith.
We cannot struggle with God; we can only cover our faces
and, like Moses, adore God (Exod. 3:6). God, who "dwells in
inaccessible light" (1 Tim. 6:16), is beyond the scope of our
understanding, however enlightened. But beyond the divine
transcendence, God is not a terrifying mystery, but full of
tenderness. God is especially close to those who are oppressed;

God hears their cry and resolves to set them free (Exod. 3:7–8). God is father of all, but most particularly father and defender of those who are oppressed and treated unjustly. Out of love for them, God takes sides, takes *their* side against the repressive measures of all the pharaohs.

This partiality on God's part shows that life and justice should be a universal guarantee to all, starting with those who are at present denied them; no one has the right to offend another human being, the image and likeness of God. God is glorified in the life-sustaining activities of men and women; God is worshiped in the doing of justice. God does not stand by impassively watching the drama of human history, in which, generally speaking, the strong impose their laws and their will on the weak. The biblical authors often present Yahweh as *Go'el,* which means: he who does justice to the weak, father of orphans and comforter of widows (see Ps. 146:9; Isa. 1:17; Jer. 7:6, 22:3; Job 29:13, 31:16).

In the experience of slavery in Egypt, which bound the Israelites together as a people, they realized their longing for liberation and witnessed to the intervention of Yahweh as liberator. The liberation from slavery in Egypt was a political event, but one that became the basis for the religious experience of full liberation—that is, liberation also from sin and death. As the bishops of Latin America said at Medellín in 1968:

> Just as formerly the first people, Israel, experienced the saving presence of God when he set them free from slavery in Egypt, so we too, the new people of God, cannot fail to feel his saving deliverance when there is real development—that is, deliverance for each and every one from less human to more human conditions of life [Introduction to Conclusions, no. 6].

Finally, the Christian God is a trinity of persons, Father, Son, and Holy Spirit. Each distinct from the other, they coexist eternally in a relationship of absolute equality and reciprocity. In the beginning there was not merely the oneness of a divine nature, but the full and perfect communion of three divine persons. This mystery provides the prototype for what society should be according to the plan of the triune God: by affirming and respecting personal individuality, it should enable persons to live in such communion and collaboration with each other as to constitute a unified society of equals and fellow citizens. The society we commonly find today, full of divisions, antagonisms, and discriminations, does not offer an environment in which we can experience the mystery of the Holy Trinity. It has to be transformed if it is to become the image and likeness of the communion of the divine persons.

3. *The kingdom is God's project in history and eternity.* Jesus Christ, second person of the Blessed Trinity, incarnated in our misery, revealed the divine plan that is to be realized through the course of history and to constitute the definitive future in eternity; the kingdom of God. The kingdom is not just in the future, for it is "in our midst" (Luke 17:21); it is not a kingdom "of this world" (John 18:36), but it nevertheless begins to come about in this world. The kingdom or reign of God means the full and total liberation of all creation, in the end, purified of all that oppresses it, transfigured by the full presence of God.

No other theological or biblical concept is as close to the ideal of integral liberation as this concept of the kingdom of God. This was well expressed by the bishops at Puebla, in the hearing of John Paul II:

There are two complementary and inseparable elements. The first is liberation from all the forms of bondage, from personal and social sin, and from everything that tears apart the human individual and society; all this finds its source in egotism, in the mystery of iniquity. The second element is liberation for progressive growth in being through communion with God and other human beings; this reaches its culmination in the perfect communion of heaven, where God is all in all and weeping forever ceases [§482; cf. *Evangelii nuntiandi*, no. 9].

Because the kingdom is the absolute, it embraces all things: sacred and profane history, the church and the world, human beings and the cosmos. Under different sacred and profane signs, the kingdom is always present where persons bring about justice, seek comradeship, forgive each other, and promote life. However, the kingdom finds a particular expression in the church, which is its perceptible sign, its privileged instrument, its "initial budding forth" and principle (see Puebla, §§227–28) insofar as it lives the gospel and builds itself up from day to day as the Body of Christ.

Seeing the kingdom as God's universal project helps us to understand the link joining creation and redemption, time and eternity. The kingdom of God is something more than historical liberations, which are always limited and open to further perfectioning, but it is anticipated and incarnated in them in time, in preparation for its full realization with the coming of the new heaven and the new earth.

4. *Jesus, the Son of God, took on oppression in order to set us free.* Jesus is God in our human misery, the Son of God become an individual Jew, at a certain time in history and in a particular social setting. The incarnation of the Word of God implies the assumption of human life as marked by the contradictions left by sin, not in order to consecrate them, but in order to redeem them. In these conditions, Jesus became a "servant" and made himself "obedient even to death on a cross" (Phil. 2:6–11; Mark 10:45). His first public word was to proclaim that the kingdom of God was "at hand" and already present as "good news" (Mark 1:14). When he publicly set out his program in the synagogue in Nazareth (Luke 4:16–21), he took on the hopes of the oppressed and announced that they were now—"this day"—being fulfilled. So the Messiah is the

one who brings about the liberation of all classes of unfortu-
nates. The kingdom is also liberation from sin (Luke 24:27;
Acts 2:38; 5:31; 13:38), but this must not be interpreted in a
reductionist sense to the point where the infrastructural dimension in Jesus' preaching stressed by the evangelists is lost
sight of.

The kingdom is not presented simply as something to be
hoped for in the future; it is already being made concrete in
Jesus' actions. His miracles and healings, besides demonstrating his divinity, are designed to show that his liberating proclamation is already being made history among the oppressed,
the special recipients of his teaching and first beneficiaries of
his actions. The kingdom is a gift of God offered gratuitously
to all. But the way into it is through the process of conversion.
The conversion demanded by Jesus does not mean just a
change of convictions (theory) but above all a change of
attitude (practice) toward all one's previous personal, social,
and religious relationships.

The liberation wrought by Jesus outside the law and customs of the time, and his radical requirements for a change of
behavior along the lines of the Beatitudes, led him into serious
conflict with all the authorities of his age. He knew defamation and demoralization, persecution and the threat of death.
His capture, torture, judicial condemnation, and crucifixion
can be understood only as a consequence of his activity and his
life. In a world that refused to listen to his message and to take
up the way of conversion, the only alternative open to Jesus as
a way of staying faithful to the Father and to his own preaching was to accept martyrdom. The cross is the expression of
the human rejection of Jesus, on the one hand, and of his
sacrificial acceptance by the Father, on the other.

The resurrection uncovers the absolute meaning of the
message of the kingdom, and of Jesus' life and death. It is the
definitive triumph of life and of hope for a reconciled kingdom in which universal peace is the fruit of divine justice and
the integration of all things in God. The resurrection has to be

seen as full liberation from all the obstacles standing in the way of the lordship of God and the full realization of all the dynamic forces for life and glory placed by God within human beings and the whole of creation.

The resurrection also, and especially, reveals the meaning of the death of the innocent, of those who are rejected for having proclaimed a greater justice—God's justice—and of all those who, like Jesus, support a good cause and are anonymously liquidated. It was not a Caesar at the height of his power who was raised from the dead, but someone destroyed by crucifixion on Calvary. Those who have been unjustly put to death in a good cause share in his resurrection.

Following Jesus means taking up his cause, being ready to bear the persecution it brings and brave enough to share his fate in the hope of inheriting the full liberation that the resurrection offers us.

5. *The Holy Spirit, "Father of the poor," is present in the struggles of the oppressed.* Like the Son, the Holy Spirit was sent into the world to further and complete the work of integral redemption and liberation. The special field of action for the Spirit is history. Like the wind (the biblical meaning of "spirit"), the Spirit is present in everything that implies movement, transformation, growth. No one and nothing is beyond the reach of the Spirit, inside and outside the Christian sphere. The Spirit takes hold of persons, fills them with enthusiasm, endows them with special charisms and abilities to change religion and society, break open rigid institutions and make things new. The Spirit presides over the religious experience of peoples, not allowing them to forget the dimension of eternity or succumb to the appeals of the flesh.

The Holy Spirit becomes a participant in the struggles and resistance of the poor in a quite special way. Not without reason is the Spirit called "Father of the poor" in the liturgy: giving them strength, day after day, to face up to the arduous struggle for their own survival and that of their families, finding the strength to put up with a socio-economic system

that oppresses them, one that they have no hope of changing
from one day to the next; helping keep alive their hope that
some things will get better and that, united, they will eventu-
ally set themselves free. Their piety, their sense of God; their
solidarity, hospitality, and fortitude; their native wisdom, fed
on suffering and experience; their love for their own children
and those of others; their capacity for celebration and joy in
the midst of the most painful conflicts; the serenity with which
they face the harshness of their struggle for life; their perception of what is possible and viable; their moderation in the use
of force and their virtually limitless powers of resistance to the
persistent, daily aggression of the socio-economic system with
its consequent social marginalization—all these qualities are
gifts of the Holy Spirit, forms of the ineffable presence and
activity of the Spirit among the oppressed.

But this activity is seen even more clearly when they rise up,
decide to take history into their own hands, and organize
themselves to bring about the transformation of society in the
direction of the dream in which there will be a place for all with
dignity and peace. The history of the struggles of the oppressed for their liberation is the history of the call of the Holy
Spirit to the heart of a divided world. It is because of the Spirit
that the ideals of equality and fellowship, the utopia of a
world in which it will be easier to love and recognize in the face
of the other the maternal and paternal features of God, will
never be allowed to die or be forgotten under the pressure of
resignation.

It is also in the light of the action of the Spirit that the
emergence of base Christian communities should be understood. More a happening than an institution, they bring into
the present the movement Jesus started and commit themselves to the justice of the kingdom of God. This is where the
church can be seen to be the sacrament of the Holy Spirit,
endowed with many charisms, ministries and services for the
good of all and the building of the kingdom in history.

6. *Mary is the prophetic and liberating woman of the*

people. The people's devotion to Mary has deep dogmatic roots: she is the Mother of God, the Immaculate Conception, the Virgin of Nazareth, and the one human being taken up into heavenly glory in all her human reality. From the standpoint of liberation, certain characteristics of hers stand out as dear to Christians of the base communities committed in the light of their faith to the transformation of society.

In the first place, all the theological greatness of Mary is based on the lowliness of her historical condition. She is Mary from Nazareth, a woman of the people, who observed the popular religious customs of the time (the presentation of Jesus in the temple and the pilgrimage to Jerusalem [Luke 2:21ff. and 41ff.]), who visited her relatives (Luke 1:39ff.), who would not miss a wedding (John 2), who worried about her son (Luke 2:48–51; Mark 3:31–32), and who followed him to the foot of the cross, as any devoted mother would have done (John 19:25). Because of this ordinariness, and not in spite of it, Mary was everything that faith proclaims her to be, for God did "great things" for her (Luke 1:49).

In the second place, Mary is the perfect example of faith and availability for God's purpose (Luke 1:45, 38). She certainly did not understand the full extent of the mystery being brought about through her—the coming of the Holy Spirit upon her and the virginal conception of the eternal Son of the Father in her womb (Luke 1:35; Matt. 1:18), but even so she trusted in God's purpose. She thinks not of herself but of others, of her cousin Elizabeth (Luke 1:39ff.), of her son lost on the pilgrimage (Luke 2:43), of those who have no wine at the marriage feast at Cana (John 2:3). Persons can be liberators only if they free themselves from their own preoccupations and place their lives at the service of others, as did Mary, Jesus, and Joseph.

In the third place, Mary is the prophetess of the Magnificat. Anticipating the liberating proclamation of her son, she shows herself attentive and sensitive to the fate of the humiliated and debased; in a context of praising God, she raises her voice in denunciation and invokes divine revolution in the relationship between oppressors and oppressed. Paul VI gave excellent expression to this whole liberating dimension of Mary in his apostolic exhortation *Marialis Cultus* of 1974:

> Mary of Nazareth, despite her total submission to the will of God, was far from being a passively submissive woman or one given to an alienating religiosity; she was a woman who had no hesitation in affirming that God is the avenger of the humble and oppressed, who pulls down the mighty of this world from their thrones (Luke 1:51–53). We can recognize in Mary, "who stands out among the poor and humble of the Lord" (LG 55), a strong woman, who knew poverty, suffering, flight, and exile (Matt. 2:13–23)—situations that cannot escape the attention of those who with an evangelical spirit seek to channel the liberating energies of man and society [no. 37].

Finally, Mary is as she appears in the popular religion of Latin America. There is no part of Latin America in which the name of Mary is not given to persons, cities, mountains, and innumerable shrines. Mary loves the poor of Latin America. She took on the dark face of the slaves and the persecuted Amerindians. She is the *Morenita* ("little dark girl") in Guadalupe, Mexico; she is Nossa Senhora da Aparecida, bound like the slaves in Brazil; she is the dark-complexioned Virgin of Charity in Cuba; the list is endless.

The masses of the poor bring their troubles to the centers of Marian pilgrimage; they dry their tears there and are filled with renewed strength and hope to carry on struggling and surviving. In these places Mary becomes "the sacramental presence of the maternal features of God" (Puebla, §291), the "ever-renewed star of evangelization" (*Evangelii nuntiandi,* no. 81), and together with Christ her son, in union with the oppressed, the "protagonist of history" (Puebla, §293).

7. *The church is sign and instrument of liberation.* The church is the inheritor in history of the mystery of Christ and his Spirit, and finds the kingdom in history as its conscious and institutionalized expression. With this, it is still a mystery of faith. It is the organized human response made by Christ's followers to God's gift; this makes it, without division or confusion, at once divine and human, sharing in the weakness of all that is human, and in the glory of all that is divine.

From the beginning of its presence in Latin American history, the church has spread its influence throughout the people. It was often an accomplice in the colonization process that entailed the disintegration of Amerindian cultures, but it has also proclaimed freedom and taken part in processes of liberation. In the last few decades, faced with the growing degradation of the lives of the masses, it has made itself conscious that its mission is one of liberating evangelization.

The best way of evangelizing the poor consists in allowing the poor themselves to become the church and help the whole church to become truly a poor church and a church of the poor. In order to accomplish this, thousands of base communities, Bible-study circles, and centers of pastoral work among the people have sprung up in virtually all parts of Latin America. In these communities Christians have been discovering *communion* as the structural and structuring theological value of the church. Rather than church-institution, organized as a "perfect society" and hierarchically structured, the church should be the community of the faithful living in comradely relationships of sharing, love, and service. These communities are better able to embody the meeting between faith and life, between the gospel and the signs of the times, understood in community, and to be a more transparent witness to Christian commitment, than are large parishes, with their more anonymous character. A vast network of base communities has sprung up, in which cardinals, bishops, priests, religious, and various forms of the lay apostolate all come together.

Despite the tensions attendant upon any living body, there is generally a good spirit of convergence between the institutional church and this wide network of base communities. They can recognize in one another the same evangelical spirit and cooperate in proclaiming the good news of Jesus and working for liberation in a divided society.

These Christian communities, united and in communion with their pastors, form the true base from which the church can become, as a matter of fact and not just of rhetoric, the people of God on pilgrimage, on its way. If they are to be the people of God, Christians have first to become a people—that is, a network of living communities working out their understandings, planning their courses of action, and organizing themselves for action. When this people enters the church through faith, baptism, and evangelical practice, it makes the church the people of God in history, which in Latin America is becoming more and more closely allied with popular culture.

This new route taken by the people of God with its new communities has created the various ministries and services necessary to attend to the religious and human needs that arise; roles and styles of pastoral ministration have been redefined, and the communities as a whole have taken on the task of evangelization.

A church thus born of the faith of the people can truly show itself as the sign of the integral liberation that the Father wills for his children, and as the proper instrument for its implementation in history. In its celebrations, popular dramatizations, ritualization of sacramental life, and its whole variety of religious creativity, it gives symbolical expression to the liberation already experienced by the people—fragile, certainly, but nevertheless true and anticipatory of the full liberation to come in the final kingdom of the Father.

8. *The rights of the poor are God's rights.* Theological reflection on the primacy of dignity of the poor, as explained in the last chapter, has helped to lead the churches to develop their concern for the defense and promotion of human rights.

Pastoral work among the poor has led to the discovery of their historical strength and sacred dignity. Part of integral evangelization consists in fostering a sense of the inviolability of individual human beings and in guaranteeing their basic rights, particularly those in the *social* sphere. The liberal-bourgeois tradition defends individual rights disconnected from society and from basic solidarity with all. Liberation theology has corrected and enriched this tradition by taking account of biblical sources. These speak primarily of the rights of the poor, of outcasts, of orphans and widows. All who are unprotected and downtrodden find their guarantor and advocate in God. God and the Messiah take on the defense of those who have no one to plead for them.

The rights of the poor are the rights of God. The struggle for promotion of human dignity and defense of threatened rights must begin with the rights of the poor. They show us the need for a certain hierarchization of rights; first must come *basic* rights, the rights to life and to the means of sustaining life (food, work, basic health care, housing, literacy); then come the other human rights: freedom of expression, of conscience, of movement, and of religion.

Throughout Latin America there are now hundreds of action groups, Justice and Peace groups, centers for the Defense of Human Rights, for example, in which the poor themselves, together with their allies (lawyers or other "organic intellectuals") make prophetic denunciations of the violations they suffer, discuss their experiences with other movements, organize resistance, and defend those accused in the courts. As the bishops at Puebla said: "The love of God . . . for us today must become first and foremost a labor of justice on behalf of the oppressed, an effort of liberation for those who are most in need of it" (§327; cf. §1145).

9. *Liberated human potential becomes liberative.* Liberation theology, which is essentially practical, has an immediate bearing on human ethics and attitudes. It has produced a new schematization of how to be Christian in the contemporary

world, as we shall show at the end of this book. Here, we want only to point out some aspects of the ethical implications.

Christians are faced with the social and structural sin of oppression and injustice under which great numbers of persons are suffering. This is the sin that festers in the institutions and structures of society, inclining individuals and groups to behavior contrary to God's purpose. Let us be clear that "structures" are not just things but forms of relatedness between things and the persons bound up with them. Overcoming social sin requires a will to transformation, to a change of structures, so that they allow for more justice and participation in their functioning. Evangelical conversion requires more than a change of heart; it also requires a liberation of social organization insofar as it produces and reproduces sinful patterns of behavior. This social conversion is brought about through transformative social struggle, with the tactics and strategy suited to bringing about the changes needed. Social sin has to be opposed by social grace, fruit of God's gift and of human endeavor inspired by God.

Charity as a form of being-for-others will always have its validity. But in the social dimension, loving means collaborating in the formation of new structures, supporting those that represent an advance in the campaign for a better quality of life, and political commitment in favor of an option for solidarity with the poor. There is a particular challenge to social love in class struggle, an aspect of the reality of a society marked by class antagonisms. By his example Jesus showed that there can be compatibility between love of others and opposition to their attitudes. We have to love others as such in whatever situation, but we also have to oppose attitudes and systems that do not conform to the ethical criteria of Jesus' message. Social peace and reconciliation are possible only to the extent that the real motives that continually provoke conflict are superseded: unequal and unjust relationships between capital and labor; racial, cultural, and sexual discrimination. So there are specific challenges to the holiness of liberative

Christians: to love without hating; to fight for the success of a just cause without being deceived by emotions; and, although respecting different opinions, being objective about one's own position and safeguarding the unity of the community.

Struggle for liberation alongside the oppressed has provoked persecutions and martyrdoms. Living the spirit of the Beatitudes in this context, accepting such consequences as a part of evangelical commitment, forces Christians to be truly free, already members of the kingdom of God, and therefore effective workers for liberation. Here the spirituality of resurrection takes on its full meaning: rather than celebrate the triumph of life, it demonstrates the victory of a crucified Liberator who, because he freely gave his life for others, inherited the fullness of God's life.

Liberative Christians unite heaven and earth, the building of the human city with the eschatological city of God, the promotion of the minimum of life in the present with the maximum of life in eternity. They reject nothing that is truly human and has therefore been taken up by the Son of God; they do everything they can toward the full liberation that will be realized when the Lord comes, to bring to its fullness all that men and women, and especially the oppressed, have brought about.

Other Challenges to Liberation Theology

Besides the key themes already listed, liberation theology faces many other challenges, specific subjects for its attention that are being studied and acted upon in the light of the intuitions and procedures proper to this type of reflection. So, for example, particularly in Central America—in view of the seriousness of the state of violence there—a "theology of life" is being worked out, in opposition to the socio-historical mechanisms of death. This has led to the associated development of a critical "theology of the economy" and "theology of politics."

Women as such are not so much a subject for study as a perspective from which all subjects can and should be examined by both men and women. Black and indigenous theologies are being worked out by these groups themselves, both collaborating with and complementing other strands of liberation theology. From the outset, of course, spirituality has been a prime concern of liberation theologians, particulary those working from within the religious orders and CLAR *(Conferencia Latinoamericana de Religiosos),* and centers of pastoral work.

Whatever the subject, the common element in the endeavor, its *tonus firmus,* is the articulation between the dogmatic content of faith and its practical and social application. The achievements of Christian faith are permanently tied to historical needs. It is this approximation and confrontation that give birth to the liberating dimension of the Christian message.

Temptations Facing Liberation Theology

Let us not pass over the temptations to which liberation theologians can be liable, temptations pointed out some time ago by critics and—at least in part—repeated by the magisterium. But at the same time it should be noted that most liberation theologians take account of these in their own work. Some of them are:

Disregard for mystical roots, from which all true commitment to liberation springs, and overemphasis of political action. It is in prayer and contemplation, and intimate and communitarian contact with God, that the motivations for a faith-inspired commitment to the oppressed and all humankind spring and are renewed.

Overstressing the political aspect of questions relating to oppression and liberation, at the expense of other, more supple and more deeply human aspects: friendship, pardon, feeling for leisure and celebration, open dialogue with everyone, sensitivity to artistic and spiritual riches.

Subordinating considerations of faith to considerations of society in one-sided constructs paying too much attention to class struggle and too little to what is specifically religious and Christian. This temptation affects exegesis and liturgy above all.

Absolutization of liberation theology, downgrading the value of other theologies, and overemphasizing the socio-economic aspects of evangelical poverty, which can lead to underemphasis on other types of social oppression, such as discrimination against blacks, women, or indigenous cultures.

Excessive stress laid on differences between liberation theology and the classic tradition of the church in ethics, ideals, and pastoral initiatives, instead of stressing points of continuity.

Lack of concern for deepening dialogue with other Christian churches or with other contemporary theologies and the doctrinal and social teachings of the universal and local magisterium, with a consequent lack of enrichment that could be derived from them to produce a more fruitful liberation theology.

Unconcern on the part of liberation theologians for making themselves intelligible to the different levels of church authority, with a consequent delay in the process of converting the church to the poor and in the ecclesiastical championing of human rights, which apply in the religious sphere as well.

The way to overcome all these temptations is for liberation theologians to become ever more strongly imbued with a sense of Christ, being "those who have the mind of Christ" (1 Cor. 2:16). They also need to be firmly linked to the ecclesial community and deeply nourished by the vigorous mystical sustenance of popular religion and faith.

Chapter 5

A Concise History
of Liberation Theology

Antecedents

The historical roots of liberation theology are to be found in the prophetic tradition of evangelists and missionaries from the earliest colonial days in Latin America—churchmen who questioned the type of presence adopted by the church and the way indigenous peoples, blacks, mestizos, and the poor rural and urban masses were treated. The names of Bartolomé de Las Casas, Antonio de Montesinos, Antonio Vieira, Brother Caneca, and others can stand for a whole host of religious personalities who have graced every century of our short history. They are the source of the type of social and ecclesial understanding that is emerging today.

Social and Political Development

The populist governments of the 1950s and 1960s—especially those of Perón in Argentina, Vargas in Brazil, and Cárdenas in Mexico—inspired nationalistic consciousness and significant industrial development in the shape of import substitution. This benefited the middle classes and urban proletariat but threw huge sectors of the peasantry into deeper rural marginalization or sprawling urban shantytowns. Development proceeded along the lines of dependent capitalism, subsidiary to that of the rich nations and excluding the great majorities of national populations. This process led to the creation of strong popular movements seeking profound changes in the socio-economic structure of their countries. These movements in turn provoked the rise of military dictatorships, which sought to safeguard or promote the interests of capital, associated with a high level of "national security" achieved through political repression and police control of all public demonstrations.

In this context the socialist revolution in Cuba stood out as an alternative leading to the dissolution of the chief cause of underdevelopment: dependence. Pockets of armed uprising appeared in many countries, aimed at overthrowing the ruling powers and installing socialist-inspired regimes. There was a great stirring for change among the popular sections of society, a truly prerevolutionary atmosphere.

Ecclesial Development

Starting in the 1960s, a great wind of renewal blew through the churches. They began to take their social mission seriously: lay persons committed themselves to work among the poor, charismatic bishops and priests encouraged the calls for progress and national modernization. Various church organizations promoted understanding of and improvements in the living conditions of the people: movements such as Young Christian Students, Young Christian Workers, Young Christian Agriculturalists, the Movement for Basic Education, groups that set up educational radio programs, and the first base ecclesial communities.

The work of these—generally middle-class—Christians was sustained theologically by the European theology of earthly realities, the integral humanism of Jacques Maritain, the social personalism of Mounier, the progressive evolutionism of

Teilhard de Chardin, Henri de Lubac's reflections on the social dimension of dogma, Yves Congar's theology of the laity, and the work of M.-D. Chenu. The Second Vatican Council then gave the best possible theoretical justification to activities developed under the signs of a theology of progress, of authentic secularization and human advancement.

The end of the 1960s, with the crisis of populism and the developmentalist model, brought the advent of a vigorous current of sociological thinking, which unmasked the true causes of underdevelopment. Development and underdevelopment are two sides of the same coin. All the nations of the Western world were engaged in a vast process of development; however, it was interdependent and unequal, organized in such a way that the benefits flowed to the already developed countries of the "center" and the disadvantages were meted out to the historically backward and underdeveloped countries of the "periphery." The poverty of Third World countries was the price to be paid for the First World to be able to enjoy the fruits of overabundance.

In ecclesial circles by now accustomed to following developments in society and studies of its problems, this interpretation acted as a leaven, yielding a new vitality and critical spirit in pastoral circles. The relationship of dependence of the periphery on the center had to be replaced by a process of breaking away and liberation. So the basis of a theology of development was undermined and the theoretical foundations for a theology of liberation were laid. Its material foundations were provided only when popular movements and Christian groups came together in the struggle for social and political liberation, with the ultimate aim of complete and integral liberation. This was when the objective conditions for an authentic liberation theology came about.

Theological Development

The first theological reflections that were to lead to liberation theology had their origins in a context of dialogue between a church and a society in ferment, between Christian faith and the longings for transformation and liberation arising from the people. The Second Vatican Council produced a theological atmosphere characterized by great freedom and creativity. This gave Latin American theologians the courage to think for themselves about pastoral problems affecting their countries. This process could be seen at work among both Catholic and Protestant thinkers with the group Church and Society in Latin America (ISAL) taking a prominent part. There were frequent meetings between Catholic theologians (Gustavo Gutiérrez, Segundo Galilea, Juan Luis Segundo, Lucio Gera, and others) and Protestant (Emilio Castro, Julio de Santa Ana, Rubem Alves, José Míguez Bonino), leading to intensified reflection on the relationship between faith and poverty, the gospel and social justice, and the like. In Brazil, between 1959 and 1964, the Catholic left produced a series of basic texts on the need for a Christian ideal of history, linked to popular action, with a methodology that foreshadowed that of liberation theology; they urged personal engagement in the world, backed up by studies of social and liberal sciences, and illustrated by the universal principles of Christianity.

At a meeting of Latin American theologians held in Petrópolis (Rio de Janeiro) in March 1964, Gustavo Gutiérrez described theology as critical reflection on praxis. This line of thought was further developed at meetings in Havana, Bogotá, and Cuernavaca in June and July 1965. Many other meetings were held as part of the preparatory work for the Medellín conference of 1968; these acted as laboratories for a theology worked out on the basis of pastoral concerns and committed Christian action. Lectures given by Gustavo Gutiérrez in Montreal in 1967 and at Chimbote in Peru on the poverty of the Third World and the challenge it posed to the development of a pastoral strategy of liberation were a further powerful impetus toward a theology of liberation. Its outlines were first put forward at the theological congress at Cartigny, Switzerland, in 1969: "Toward a Theology of Liberation."

The first Catholic congresses devoted to liberation theology were held in Bogotá in March 1970 and July 1971. On the Protestant side, ISAL organized something similar in Buenos Aires the same years.

Finally, in December 1971, Gustavo Gutiérrez published his seminal work, *Teología de la liberación*. In May Hugo Assmann had conducted a symposium, "Oppression-Liberation: The Challenge to Christians," in Montevideo, and Leonardo Boff had published a series of articles under the title *Jesus Cristo Libertador* (see the Bibliography for details on these and other basic works). The door was opened for the development of a theology from the periphery dealing with the concerns of this periphery, concerns that presented and still present an immense challenge to the evangelizing mission of the church.

Formulation

For the sake of clarity and a better understanding of the advances made, the formulation of liberation theology can be divided into four stages.

The Foundational Stage

The foundations were laid by those who sketched the general outlines of this way of doing theology. Besides the all-important writings of Gustavo Gutiérrez, outstanding works were produced by Juan Luis Segundo: *De la sociedad a la teología* (1970), *Liberación de la teología* (1975); by Hugo Assmann: *Teología desde la praxis de liberación* (1973); Lucio Gera: *Apuntes para una interpretación de le Iglesia argentina* (1970), *Teología de la liberación* (1973). Others who should be mentioned are Bishop (later Cardinal) Eduardo Pironio, secretary of CELAM, Segundo Galilea, and Raimundo Caramuru, principal theological consultant to the Brazilian Bishops' Conference. There was also a great ferment of activity in the shape of courses and retreats during this period.

On the Protestant side, besides Emilio Castro and Julio de

Santa Ana, the outstanding contributions were made by Rubem Alves: *Religion: Opium of the People or Instrument of Liberation* (1969), and José Míguez Bonino: *La fe en busca de eficacia* (1967) and *Doing Theology in a Revolutionary Situation* (1975).

Lay persons such as Héctor Borrat, Methol Ferré, and Luiz Alberto Gómez de Souza did valuable work in linking theology with the social sciences, as did the Belgian priest François Houtart and the Chilean G. Arroyo.

The Building Stage

The first stage was characterized by the presentation of liberation theology as a sort of "fundamental theology"—that is, as an opening up of new horizons and perspectives that gave a new outlook on the whole of theology. The second stage moved on to the first efforts at giving the liberation approach doctrinal content. Three areas received most attention as corresponding to the most urgent needs in the life of the church: spirituality, christology, and ecclesiology. There was a wide range of publications from many Latin American countries. The main writers: in Argentina, Enrique Dussel, Juan Carlos Scannone, Severino Croatto, and Aldo Büntig; in Brazil, João Batista Libânio, Frei Betto, Carlos Mesters, José Comblin, Eduardo Hoornaert, José Oscar Beozzo, Gilberto Gorgulho, Carlos Palácio, Leonardo Boff; in Chile, Ronaldo Muñoz, Sergio Torres, and Pablo Richard; in Mexico, Raúl Vidales, Luis del Valle, Arnaldo Zenteno, Camilo Maccise, and Jesús García; in Central America, Ignacio Ellacuría, Jon Sobrino, Juan H. Pico, Uriel Molina; in Venezuela, Pedro Trigo and Otto Maduro (sociologist); in Colombia, Luis Patiño and Cecilio de Llora.

The Settling-in Stage

With the process of theological reflection well advanced, the need was seen for a dual process of "settling in" if the theology of liberation was to become firmly established. On the one hand was the understanding that the theological current needed to be given a firm epistemological basis: how to avoid duplications and confusions of language and levels while giving coherent expression to the themes arising from original spiritual experience, taking in the analytical *seeing* stage, moving on to the theological *judging* stage, and so to the pastoral *action* stage? Good liberation theology presupposes the art of linking its theories with the explicit inclusion of practice; in this area liberation theology found fruitful collaborators, not only for its own purposes, but for those of the overall theological process. On the other hand, the "settling in" process was effectively achieved through the deliberate mingling of theologians and other intellectuals in popular circles and processes of liberation.

More and more theologians became pastors too, militant agents of inspiration for the life of the church at its grass roots and those of society. It became usual to see theologians taking part in involved epistemological discussions in learned congresses, then leaving to go back to their bases among the people to become involved in matters of catechesis, trade union politics, and community organization.

Names again are many; a selection should include Antônio A. da Silva, Rogério de Almeida Cunha, Clodovis Boff, Hugo d'Ans, Francisco Taborda, Marcelo de Barros, and Eliseu Lopes, all from Brazil; Elsa Tamez and Victorio Araya from Costa Rica; D. Irarrazaval, Carmen Llora, Riolando Ames, R. Antoncich, and the late Hugo Echegaray, from Peru; Víctor Codina from Bolivia; Virgilio Elizondo from Texas; J. L. Caravia from Ecuador; P. Läennec from Haiti.

The Formalization Stage

Any original theological vision tends, with the passage of time and through its own internal logic, to seek more formal expression. Liberation theology always set out to reexamine the whole basic content of revelation and tradition so as to bring out the social and liberating dimensions implicit in both sources. Again, this is not a matter of reducing the totality of mystery to this one dimension, but of underlining aspects of a greater truth particularly relevant to our context of oppression and liberation.

Such a formalization also corresponds to pastoral requirements. The last few years have seen a great extension of situations in which the church has become involved with the oppressed, with a very large number of pastoral workers involved. Many movements have come into being under the tutelage, to a large extent, of liberation theology; these in turn have posed new challenges to liberation theology. In Brazil alone, there are movements or centers for black unity and conscientization, human rights, defense of slum-dwellers, marginalized women, mission to Amerindians, rural pastoral strategy, and so forth—all concerned in one way or another with the poorest of the poor seeking liberation.

To cope with this broad pastoral need and give theological underpinning to the training of pastoral workers, a group of more than one hundred Catholic theologians (with ecumenical contacts and Protestant collaborators) have been planning a series of fifty-five volumes under the heading *Theology and Liberation*, with Portuguese and Spanish publication starting in late 1985 and translations into other languages planned. Its aim will be to cover all the basic themes of theology and pastoral work from a liberation viewpoint. There are too many persons involved at this stage to list them here: all those from the earlier stages would be included, together with a number of new collaborators.

Support and Opposition

Liberation theology spread by virtue of the inner dynamism with which it codified Christian faith as it applies to the pastoral needs of the poor. Meetings, congresses, theological reviews, and the support of prophetic bishops—Hélder Câmara, Luis Proaño, Samuel Ruiz, Sergio Méndez Arceo, and Cardinals Paulo Evaristo Arns and D. A. Lorscheider, among many others—have helped to give it weight and credibility.

A series of events has been instrumental in spreading this theology and ensuring its "reception" among theologians the world over:

• The congress at El Escorial, Spain, in July 1972 on the subject of "Christian faith and the transformation of society in Latin America."

• The first congress of Latin American theologians, held in Mexico City in August 1975.

• The first formal contacts between liberation theologians and advocates of U.S. black liberation and other liberation movements—feminist, Amerindian, and the like.

• The creation of the Ecumenical Association of Third World Theologians (EATWOT) in 1976 and the congresses it has held: Dar es Salaam in 1976, Accra in 1977, Wennappuwa, Sri Lanka, in 1979, São Paulo in 1980, Geneva in 1983, Oaxtepec, Mexico, in 1986. All these produced Final Conclusions with their particular characteristics, but all within the framework of liberation theology.

• Finally, the international theological review *Concilium* (published in seven languages) devoted a complete issue (vol. 6, no. 10, June 1974) to the subject of liberation theology, with all the articles coming from Latin American liberation theologians.

A number of important reviews in Latin America have become regular vehicles for the publication of articles and discussions by liberation theologians: in Mexico, *Christus, Servir,* and *Contacto*; in Venezuela, *SIC*; in Chile, *Pastoral Popular*; in Brazil, *Revista Eclesiástica Brasileira* (REB), *Grande Sinal, Puebla,* and *Perspectiva Teológica*; in El Salvador, *Estudios Centroamericanos* (ECA) and *Revista Latinoamericana de Teología*; in Panama, *Diálogo Social.*

Most countries in Latin America also have centers for theological and pastoral studies: CEAS (*Centro de Estudos e Ação*, Salvador), CEP (*Centro de Estudios y Publicaciones*, Lima), ITER (*Instituto de Teologia do Recife*), DEI (*Departmento Ecuménico de Investigaciones*, San José, Costa Rica), CAV (*Centre Antonio Valdivieso*, Managua), and many more. They have been important for training students imbued with a liberation approach.

While all these developments were taking place, reservations and opposition began to be expressed by some who feared the faith was becoming overpoliticized, and by others who mistrusted any use of Marxist categories in analyzing social structures. Also many were unable to accept the deep changes in the structure of capitalist society postulated by this theology. This negative reaction crystalized around three figures in particular: Alfonso López Trujillo, formerly secretary and later president of CELAM, Roger Vekemans of CEDIAL (*Centro de Estudios para el Desarrollo e Integración de América Latina,* Bogotá) and the review *Tierra Nueva,* and Bonaventura Kloppenburg, formerly director of the Medellín Pastoral Institute, later auxiliary bishop of Salvador, Brazil, and author of *Christian Salvation and Human Temporal Progress* (1979).

The Magisterium of the Church

As a general rule, the magisterium watches the development of new theologies with close attention but rarely intervenes and then only with great caution and discreet support or opposition.

As far back as 1971, the final document "Justice in the World," the topic of the second ordinary assembly of the Synod of Bishops, already showed traces of liberation theology. Its echoes had become much stronger by 1974, at the third assembly of the Synod, on "Evangelization of the Modern World." The following year, Paul VI devoted fifteen paragraphs of his apostolic exhortation *Evangelii nuntiandi* to the relationship between evangelization and liberation (nos. 25–39). This discussion forms the central core of the document, and without attempting to summarize the pope's position, we can just say that it is one of the most profound, balanced, and theological expositions yet made of the longing of the oppressed for liberation.

The magisterium has also produced the "Instruction on Some Aspects of Liberation Theology," under the auspices of the Prefect and Secretariat of the Congregation for the Doctrine of the Faith, dated August 6, 1984, and published September 3. The main points about this document are its legitimation of the expression and purpose of liberation theology, and its warning to Christians of the risk inherent in an uncritical acceptance of Marxism as a dominant principle in theological endeavor. The subject had been studied in Rome since 1974, and had been the concern of innumerable sessions of the International Theological Commission, though it did not publish any results until 1977, when it produced a "Declaration on Human Development and Christian Salvation" (included as an appendix in Kloppenburg's book mentioned above), which shows a grasp of the questions such as was to be expected from such an august theological body.

The magisterium of the church in Latin America has expressed itself primarily through the documents of two conferences. The second general conference of the episcopate of Latin America, held at Medellín, Colombia, in 1968, spoke of the church "listening to the cry of the poor and becoming the interpreter of their anguish"; this was the first flowering of the theme of liberation, which began to be worked out systematically only after Medellín. The third general conference, held at Puebla, Mexico, in 1979, shows the theme of liberation running right through its final document. The liberation dimension is seen as an "integral part" (§§355, 1254, 1283) of the mission of the church, "indispensable" (§§562, 1270), "essential" (§1302). A large part of the document (§§470–506) is devoted to evangelization, liberation, and human promotion, and a whole chapter (§§1134–56) to the "preferential option for the poor," a central axis of liberation theology.

The general tenor of the pronouncements of the magisterium, whether papal or coming from the Synod of Bishops, has been to recognize the positive aspects of liberation theology, especially with reference to the poor and the need for their liberation, as forming part of the universal heritage of Christian commitment to history. Criticisms of certain tendencies within liberation theology, which have to be taken into account, do not negate the vigorous and healthy nucleus of this form of Christian thinking, which has done so much to bring the message of the historical Jesus to the world of today.

Chapter 6

Liberation Theology Worldwide

Liberation theology has been called an "infant theology." It is certainly young: born in the early 1970s. Yet there is no denying that it has already made its presence felt worldwide. This chapter aims at providing a brief sketch of its worldwide presence in three broad areas: theology, the institutional church, and social and political issues.

A Dynamic and Inspiring Theology

Among theological currents in the churches today, there is no doubt that liberation theology stands out as having particular dynamism. The roots of this dynamism are to be found much more in popular movements, in society, and in the local churches with which it is associated than in theology itself. Because its subject matter is relevant and specific, its writings are read in very wide circles, particularly by those who are engaged in pastoral work among the very poor.

Here, however, we are confining ourselves rather to professional liberation theology and its spread through the professional theological field, leaving aside its pastoral and popular expressions. These expressions, it goes without saying, are strongly present in many institutes of higher education, in seminaries and training centers for pastoral workers, and lie behind the pastoral approach of innumerable local churches and even some national ones.

Let us now see how liberation theology relates to the wider field of universal theological endeavor: in the Third World, and in the First and Second, respectively.

In the Third World

There is no doubt that Latin America and the Caribbean are the areas where the influence of liberation theology has been most strongly felt, to the point where it has become virtually synonymous with "Latin American theology." This is readily understandable: it came to birth there, and there found the fruitful soil of peoples the vast majority of whom were both Christian and oppressed, and of a church seeking to march with this people on the road to liberation.

The strength of liberation theology varies from country to country, though it is present in all. In some it is relatively weak; in others strong—Peru, Chile, Mexico, Brazil, Central America.

The Latin American Confederation of Religious (CLAR) has become a major arena for elaboration and experience of the great intuitions of liberation theology, especially as it affects the religious life. The same is true of many national religious conferences, particularly that of Brazil.

Three major scholarly institutes that support the basic orientation of liberation theology should be mentioned: CEHILA, the Commission for Studies in Latin American Church History; CEBI, the Center for Biblical Studies; and CESEP, the Ecumenical Center for Service and Evangelization of the People. CEHILA has undertaken the vast task of rewriting the whole history of Latin America and the Caribbean from the viewpoint of the poor—from a liberation perspective, that is—and several volumes of this huge project have already been published. CEBI promotes studies, courses, and publications that re-present the Bible in a liberating and popular sense. In Brazil it has a network of more than fifteen regional centers, rooted in the base communities in different parts of Brazil, whose object is to encourage widespread reading of the Bible among the people and the training of "people's exegetes." It is currently publishing a series of "people's commentaries" on the whole Bible. CESEP is an ecumenical institute which trains qualified agents from all over Latin America and the Caribbean in liberating pastoral work. There are also other ecumenical organizations inspired by liberation theology, such as CEDI (the Ecumenical Center for Dissemination and Information), in Brazil, ISAL (Church and Society in Latin America), and others.

In addition, other religious bodies, such as Catholic publishers (Vozes, Paulinas, Loyola, DEI, CRT, etc.), act as vehicles for the production and dissemination of liberation theology. It is *in* and *with* all these bodies that this theology develops, enriching them and being enriched by them in its turn.

The main areas of concern of Latin American and Caribbean liberation theology are, as we have seen, concern for the socio-economically poor and their struggle for liberation. This approach is being developed in dialogue with fraternal theologies, particularly from Africa and Asia, whose accents—as we shall see—are different, but always complementary.

Africa has a liberation theology with its own sources. Since the Second Vatican Council (and even earlier), African theologians have been reflecting on the need for cultural integration of faith and the church on the continent of Africa. Their exchanges with Latin American theology have only served to enrich an already established indigenous current of thought. African liberation theology is particulary well rooted in Zaire, Tanzania, Ghana, and South Africa. In South Africa the part played by the churches in the struggle against apartheid is well known. Here "black liberation theology" and "contextual theology" are the most deeply committed currents in the struggle. They are in regular contact with both black liberation theology in the U.S.A., and with Latin American theology. Latin American theology in turn has benefited from African theology, which has forced it to more basic thinking about cultural and racial phenomena.

Asia too has its own process of liberation thinking, particularly in India, Korea, the Philippines, Sri Lanka, and Pakistan. Here the main accent is on establishing a fruitful dialogue between Christianity and the other great religions of the area, with a view to awakening their huge potential for social liberation. Particularly at the outset, Asiatic theology took its inspiration from Latin America, whose theology it has in turn enriched through its sensitivity to the values of the great Eastern religions and especially to their strongly mystical bent.

In the First World

First world theologians have also woken up to the confrontation between Christian faith and the contradictions specific to so-called advanced societies. Thus black liberation theology has become firmly established in the U.S.A., deeply committed to the civil rights campaign waged by American blacks.

There is also a European theology of liberation developing under the direct influence of Latin American theology, particularly lively in Spain. This European liberation theology is concerned with the responsibilities of the First World with regard to the Third, with the problems of the "new poor" of advanced industrial societies (young drug addicts, the institutionalized elderly, migrant workers), not to mention questions such as ecology and nuclear energy.

The influence of feminist liberation theology—produced, naturally, by women theologians—is widespread throughout the First World. This theology sees women's liberation as an integral dimension of overall liberation, and is taking ever-increasing account of the close links that exist between sexual and economic oppression, and therefore of the political power of a feminist movement based on majority classes. It has the further tasks of trying to eliminate the sexist elements in traditional theology and rethinking the whole of faith from a feminine standpoint.

There is also the growing influence of liberation theology in the underdeveloped pockets of the First World, such as the thirty million persons of Hispanic origin in the United States, especially Mexican-Americans and Mexican immigrants.

In general, however, the way Latin American theology is making an increasing impact in theological, ecclesial, and cultural circles in the First World is through translations of books and discussions held in a large number of cultural congresses and institutes. Symptomatic of this is the number of young persons taking doctorates at famous European universities—Louvain, Paris, Salamanca, Rome, Tübingen, Münster—who choose themes connected with liberation theology for their doctoral theses.

In the Second World, the Socialist Bloc

There is little known about the state of theological thinking in this area, and still less about possible developments along the lines or influence of liberation theology. Just a few echoes come through, such as the Russian Orthodox Metropolitan Filaret's comment that the Roman document on liberation theology shows Rome to be afraid of it because it is afraid of socialism.

There is also the fact that seventy theologians from socialist countries met with a group of theologians from Latin America in Matanzas, Cuba, in January 1979, to discuss the social responsibilities of the Christian faith faced with challenges of our time.

As a final note to this section, it should be said that liberation theology, rather than trying to invade the field of universal theology, has been waking up to its proper function, which is to meditate on faith in history. So we are not here dealing so much with one theological current influencing others or even recolonizing them, nor with one particular theology engaging in dialogue with others within an ill-defined "theological pluralism." It is rather a question of a movement of the whole of theology, albeit with varied emphases, energizing and influencing all theologies. To put it succinctly: liberation theology is not a *theological movement,* but *theology in movement.* Latin American theology is therefore not so much a source or focal point of liberation theology as, more modestly, a humble catalyst and relatively dynamic element in this universal current. But until its central inspiration has been incorporated into theology as a whole, liberation theology has to appear as a particular current, devoted to what its name implies, distinct from other currents and programmatic in character. But even at this stage it is open to all theology and conscious of the fact that its final destiny is to disappear as a particular theology and become simply theology.

A Theology with an Impact

This section deals with the impact of liberation theology on the church as institution, from its highest levels down to its bases.

On the Universal Level

Starting out in Latin America, the concerns of liberation theology soon reached the highest levels of the Catholic Church, particularly during and since the 1974 Synod of Bishops, as we saw in the preceding chapter. Today the language of the poor and of liberation has become an integral part of papal pronouncements and of those of the ecclesiastical magisterium as a whole.

The Vatican document on liberation theology had the effect of bringing it to the attention of a wide public throughout the world, and producing a real "boom" in discussion of it throughout the universal church. Investigations into the works of Leonardo Boff and Gustavo Gutiérrez likewise had the effect of spreading interest in their type of theology.

Other Christian churches have also become involved in discussion of liberation theology, particularly in assemblies of the World Council of Churches, such as the fourth general assembly at Uppsala in 1968, the Bangkok assembly in 1973 on "Salvation Today," and the fifth general assembly in Nairobi in 1975.

Liberation theology has certainly moved beyond being a regional theology and is increasingly becoming a universal theology—that is, a truly "ecumenical" and "catholic" theology.

On the Regional Level

As the documents mentioned in the previous chapter show, since the Medellín conference of 1968 the bishops of Latin America have been absorbing the message of liberation theology to the extent that it now, to a greater or lesser degree, impregnates the fields of preaching, liturgy, catechesis, spirituality, and even literary and artistic expression. There is no denying that, since Puebla, the Latin American bishops' conference, CELAM, has had some difficulty in taking a detached view of the liberation project and in understanding its import: as we have seen, there is opposition to it in some circles.

As for the churches in individual countries, the situation varies: some bishops' conferences are against it, some are undecided, and others have adopted a sympathetic approach, welcoming its positive contributions, although making constructive criticism. Brazil is probably the country where the attitude of the bishops as a whole has been most closely in harmony with liberation theology, finding its spiritual orientation close to their own prophetic approach.

On the Base Level

This is where liberation theology is most present and alive. Not that it has penetrated them: these Christian communities have not had a theology imposed on them from outside or above. By no means. But it has been these communities—leaders and members—that have begun to reflect on their faith in a liberating spirit. The special contribution made by professional liberation theology has been to increase—or at most, to awaken—the spirit of theological-liberative reflection shared by pastors and faithful. There is no doubt that liberation theology on all its levels is the mode of thinking about faith that is having the most lively and enriching effect on the pastoral practices and religious life of the churches in general.

As we have seen earlier, liberation theologians have, at the urgent request of bishops, religious, and lay persons, acted as advisors at pastoral councils, general chapters of religious congregations, national and regional meetings of socio-pastoral agencies concerned with slum-dwellers, blacks, women, indigenes, to the point where one can say that theology inspires pastoral work as much as pastoral work inspires theology.

A Public and Prophetic Theology

Liberation theology has spread beyond the boundaries of the church and today is in the public domain. Why? Because it deals with issues that affect the whole of society. Let us take a quick look at this on the civil and political levels.

On the Civil Level

The Vatican document on liberation theology had the effect of increasing still further the already widespread and growing public interest in this theology. Liberation theology is now considered news by all the communications media. It is a subject of discussion in universities, trade unions, and all sorts of scholarly and political institutes. It is a subject of conversation in families, in bars and cafés, on street corners, to an extent that recalls the early church, where the population as a whole was passionately concerned in the theological debates of the time.

On the Political Level

Because of the political implications of a liberating Christianity, governments in various parts of the world have felt the need to take up positions either for or against liberation theology.

Alarm bells have rung most loudly in the United States. In 1969 President Nixon sent Nelson Rockefeller to Latin America to investigate the situation. His report stated that the church there was changing into "a force devoted to change, by revolutionary means if necessary." The Report of the Rand Corporation, made at the request of the State Department in 1972, came to the same conclusion. Better known is the Santa Fe Document, produced by advisors to President Reagan in 1982, which explicitly states: "American foreign policy must begin to counterattack (and not just react against) liberation theology." In order to put this into effect, the Institute for Religion and Democracy (IRD) was set up in the United States, with the aim (among others) of mounting an ideological campaign against Latin American liberation theology. A Catholic theologian at this institute has stated: "Events in Iran and Nicaragua began to show political analysts that it is dangerous, when making their calculations, to omit the religious factor, particularly the ideas of theologians."

As for the authoritarian regimes of Latin America, Enrique Dussel has remarked that liberation theologians are more of a threat to them than are militant communists. And the German theologian Karl Rahner commented, as did Gustavo Gutiérrez, that being a liberation theologian in Latin America today is tantamount to being a candidate for martyrdom.

There is little information on any possible influence in the Socialist bloc, though we do know that members of the Moscow Academy of Sciences have discussed the topic of Latin American liberation theology with interest.

It is worth noting that Fidel Castro is devoting considerable attention to the political and ethical significance of Latin American liberation theology, regarding its arguments as far more persuasive than those of Marxism itself. He is known to be personally studying and discussing the works of its principal authors.

With regard to militant Marxist groups in Latin America and elsewhere, it is enough here to say that liberation theology has shown:

• that Marxism no longer has a monopoly on historical change: Christians have adopted this cause in the name of their faith and have done so without taking up combative or polemical stances;

• that the Christian appeal to social commitment is meeting with a special response among the religious masses of Latin America, and demonstrating a power to communicate that the traditional revolutionary ideologies have been losing to an ever-increasing extent;

• that Christian faith is freeing itself, irreversibly, from the shackles of capitalism, which can now no longer count on the church as one of the pillars of its ideological framework; on the contrary, it is now being surprised by frontal assaults delivered from the heart of the Christian faith.

To repeat the statement of an eminent Italian Catholic politician and intellectual: liberation theology provides the most convincing refutation of modern atheism, because it has demonstrated, through its actions, that God is no longer a source of alienation in history, but the fountainhead of social commitment.

The Historical Significance of Liberation Theology

All that has been said above leads to certain conclusions about the extent to which liberation theology overflows the confines of the traditional field of theology and affects humanity itself.

1. Liberation theology is the first theology worked out on the periphery on the basis of questions raised by the periphery but with universal implications. It is the articulated cry of the oppressed, of the new barbarians beating at the gates of the empire of plenty of the nations of the center, demanding humanity, solidarity, and the opportunity to live in dignity and peace. Today, such objectives can be achieved only after a harsh struggle for liberation, to which Christian faith seeks to make its contribution.

2. Liberation theology puts on the agenda for discussion questions that concern all human beings, whatever their ideological bent or religious adherence. They concern all those who still have a spark of humanity left for considering the problems of the millions and millions of poor persons, of international justice, of the future for the wretched of the earth.

3. There is a prophetic call coming from liberation theology, in that it denounces the causes that produce oppression, and inspires an outpouring of generosity destined to overcome destructive relationships and build freedom for everyone.

4. Liberation theology belongs to contemporary history; it does not shut itself up in splendid isolation but operates on the level of everyday life, where the fate of the individual is decided; there it seeks to take on the cause of the least of all, not fearing the most rending conflicts in its efforts to guarantee at least the minimal requirements of human dignity, human life.

5. Liberation theology forces theologians to think in terms of specific actions, of the real problems of life and of the

community of faith, instead of the classic themes established by theological tradition. This means they have to be dynamic and reject immature syntheses and artificial constructs.

6. Liberation theology gives the gospel back its credibility, because it mediates an atmosphere of joy springing from sacrifices made for the sake of the weakest, from God's promise of justice for the poor and life for the downtrodden. It is by nature a popular theology, for the masses of the oppressed are its most congenial recipients and most of them understand its language and embrace its aims. For them, it is what keeps alive Jesus Christ's utopic promise of a loving, comradely world, where it is possible for God to "pitch a tent" among ordinary men and women.

7. Liberation theology sets out to be the servant of the "faith that works through charity," inspired by hope. Therefore it should be judged by the criterion by which all true theology should be judged, as St. Augustine and St. Thomas Aquinas frequently repeat: the only subjects of this science are what generate, nourish, defend, and strengthen saving and liberating faith (*De Trinitate,* c. 1; *Summa Theol.,* q. 1, a. 2).

Chapter 7

From out of the Oppressed: A New Humanity

Liberation: The Evocative Power of a Word

Liberation is "the powerful and irresistible aspiration of the poor" and "one of the principal signs of the times" (Instruction, *Libertatis nuntius*, n. 1). It defines the spirit of our epoch, of the times in which we live. Modern humankind is in quest of liberation, of a "liberated" life, which for the poor has to come through the humble sacraments of bread, a roof over their heads, health, peace.

"Liberation" is an "evangelical" term in the original sense of the word: a life-giving word, good news, a joyful announcement. The prophets spoke of *shalom,* meaning security, reconciliation, fullness, and peace. Jesus for his part spoke of the "kingdom," meaning the complete reversal of alienation, total change, sovereign life, the life "to the full" willed by God. "Liberation" should have the same power to touch, enchant, and fascinate us as Jesus' original good news. It seeks to rekindle his flame, to fan the fire he brought to earth (Luke 12:49).

"Liberation" is an evocative word, full of resonances. In it the dimensions of the spiritual and the political, the historical

90

and the ultrahistorical, are fused without losing their identity. A word open, then, to above—to divine transcendence—and to below—to earth's immanence. A word at once joyous and serious. Like the idea of Jesus' kingdom, in which the salvation of the whole person and the whole world are found together, without division.

"Liberation" is a word that today describes the program of a theology that thinks as awakened faith, that has shaken off the burden of "religion—opium of the people," that seeks a faith free from alienation, the leaven of a new history.

An Appeal to All Theologies

Liberation theology today, as a theology for the times, *our* times, works on the question of social and historical liberation within the larger framework of integral—human and divine— liberation. This is where it places its stress; this is the meaning it seeks to extract: historical liberation seen as a stage in the great process of overall liberation.

The stress on social liberation is not immediately related to integral liberation, but to other stages of integral liberation: the individual and eschatological dimensions. It contrasts political liberation and Christian liberation, and identifies a subsidiary relationship between them: the former is one aspect of the latter.

This is why liberation theology as it exists at present does not claim to be an absolute, everlasting, or perennial theology. It seeks and hopes for the ending of the oppression and poverty that are now the objects of its study. It is therefore a historical theology, very much of its time. This means that its applicability, although not transhistorical, is not merely transient, a thing of fashion; it covers a historical period, and this period will last for decades if not centuries.

Nor is it a partial theology, one more theological treatise to add to so many others. It is a whole theology, thought out in terms of today. As a result, its subject matter embraces the whole body of theological investigation, unraveling the historical-liberative dimension of each aspect, as we saw in chapter 4, above. This is why it launches an appeal to all theologians, of the First, Second, and Third World, calling on them to work out the social-liberative dimension of faith. And it is a once-and-for-all appeal: once theology as a whole has assimilated this call and made it its own, then the name "liberation theology" can be dropped, because by then all theologies will be liberation theologies in their own way—otherwise they will not be Christian theologies.

Banner of a New Society

The banner of liberation theology, firmly set in biblical ground, waves in the winds of history. Its message is that today the history of faith is embarking on its third great period, the period of construction. In the past, faith has performed a *contestatory* function: this was in the first centuries, the times of the church of the apostles, martyrs, and virgins. Then, in the post-Constantinian era, faith performed a *conservatory* function in society, *consecrating* the status quo and collaborating with the powers of the world. Today, faith has decidedly taken on a *constructive* function, contesting the existing order—thereby referring back to the early church—but also taking a longer-range view—that is, taking on its responsibility in history, which is to persuade society to conform to the utopia of the kingdom.

Consequently, liberation theology longs and fights for a new society in this world: an alternative society to capitalism, but really alternative and therefore going beyond socialism as it exists today, embodying the hopes and needs of the least of all peoples and their intrinsic potential, a project with ample resonances in the tradition of faith. And in Latin America, the one area of the world whose population is both Christian and oppressed, liberation theology has realized that it cannot lose this unique opportunity of saying a new word in history; it cannot just follow the paths trodden by other societies: it knows where they lead.

Starting from the absolute utopia of the kingdom, faith can contribute by marking out new paths to a new society—an alternative to capitalism *and* socialism—a fuller and more humane society, free and liberated, a society of the freed. But liberation theology knows that the price of this project is commitment to the process of bringing it about.

The Dream of a Truly Free Society

Liberation theology has a spirituality at its roots and a dream of its final aim: that of a society of freed men and women. Without a dream, men and women will not mobilize themselves to transform society, nor will society seek to renew its foundations. Christians believe that such a dream belongs to the realm of reality, for they have seen it realized in anticipation by Jesus Christ, who "has broken down . . . enmity . . . , so as to create . . . a single new humanity in himself, thereby making peace" (Eph. 2:14–15).

What are the main characteristics of the men and women who work to bring about the dream of this society of the freed? This is what they and its members will be like:

• *Comradely.* Like the good Samaritan, they will converge on the fallen to take them with them. There will be no liberation struggle they do not make their own, determining what sort of support they can give and how they can identify with the consequences of their actions, however burdensome they may be.

• *Prophetic.* They denounce mechanisms that generate oppression. They seek out hidden interests sheltering behind the plans of ruling powers. They proclaim the ideal of a society of equals through words and deeds. They never compromise with the truth.

• *Committed.* Action imbued with correct understanding transforms reality. So commitment to the oppressed for their liberation is worthy of the name only when it is realized along a road traveled together with others who share the same dream, expend their energies in achieving it, and are prepared to lay down their lives for it.

• *Free.* They seek freedom *from* the schemes and illusions imposed by the dominant system, in order to be free to create, with others, more adequate forms of life, of work, of being Christian; seeking freedom *from* themselves so as to be freer and more available *to* others and ready even to die in witness to the kingdom of God and its justice, becoming history in the noble struggle of the oppressed for God-given dignity, rights, and life.

• *Joyful.* The clear option for the poor and their liberation raises conflicts. The efforts required to bring about the insurrection of the gospel in oneself, in the structures of society, and in the church, often produce tensions and painful separations. Accepting such situations joyfully as the price to be paid for integral liberation is a sign of maturity and characteristic of the spirit of the Beatitudes, as so many Christians committed to the poor have shown in so many ways.

• *Contemplative.* In the midst of struggle, they do not lose the sense of the gratuitous, the value proper to every dimension of human existence—love, celebration, fellowship, communion. They will be able, like Jesus, to pray with a clear heart, to contemplate God in human history, especially in the struggles and resistance of the poor and lowly. They will appreciate the ingenuousness of children as much as the courage of fighters, and will know how to be magnanimous, without being servile, toward their adversaries.

• *Utopian.* They will not rest after advances, or be disheartened after setbacks. They will translate the eschatological hope of the kingdom for the full freedom of the children of God into historical hopes in the personal and social spheres—in work, health, culture. Those committed to integral liberation will keep in their hearts the *little utopia* of at least one meal for everyone every day, the *great utopia* of a society free from exploitation and organized around the participation of all, and finally the *absolute utopia* of communion with God in a totally redeemed creation.

The holy city, the new Jerusalem that comes down from heaven (Rev. 21:2), can be established on earth only when men and women filled with faith and passion for the gospel, united with each other, and hungry and thirsty for justice, create the human dispositions and material conditions for it. But the earth will not then be the same earth, neither will the heavens be the same heavens; they will be a *new* heaven and a *new* earth. The old earth with its oppressions will have passed away. The new earth will be a gift of God and the fruit of human effort. What was begun in history will continue in eternity: the kingdom of the freed, living as brothers and sisters in the great house of the Father.

Select Bibliography

Araya, Victorio. *El Dios de los pobres.* San José, Costa Rica: Sebila, 1983. (Engl. trans., *The God of the Poor: The Mystery of God in Latin American Liberation Theology.* Maryknoll, N.Y.: Orbis, 1987.)

Assmann, Hugo. *Teología desde la praxis de liberación. Ensayo teológico desde América Latina dependiente.* Salamanca: Sígueme, 1973. (Engl. trans., *Theology for a Nomad Church.* Maryknoll, N.Y.: Orbis, 1975; *Practical Theology of Liberation.* London: Search, 1975.)

Beozzo, J. O. *Historia da Igreja no Brasil. Ensaio de interpretação a partir do povo.* Petrópolis: Vozes, 1980.

Betto, Frei. *O que é comunidade eclesial de base.* São Paulo, 1981.

———. *Fidel e a religião. Conversas com Frei Betto.* São Paulo, 1985.

———. *Oração na ação.* Rio de Janeiro, 1977.

Boff, Clodovis. *Teologia e práctica.* Petrópolis: Vozes, 1978. (Engl. trans., *Theology and Praxis: Epistemological Foundations.* Maryknoll, N.Y.: Orbis, 1987.)

Boff, Leonardo. *Jesus Cristo Libertador.* Petrópolis: Vozes, 1971. (Engl. trans., *Jesus Christ Liberator.* Maryknoll, N.Y.: Orbis, 1978.)

———, and Boff, Clodovis. *Da libertação.* Petrópolis, Vozes: 1979. (Engl. trans., *Salvation and Liberation.* Maryknoll, N.Y.: Orbis/Blackburn, Australia, 1984.)

———, and Boff, Clodovis. *Teologia da libertação no debate atual.* Petrópolis: Vozes, 1985.

Bonino, José Míguez. *Doing Theology in a Revolutionary Situation.* Philadelphia: Fortress, 1975.

————. *La fe en busca de eficacia*. 1967.

Bonnín, E. *Espiritualidad y liberación en América Latina*. San José, Costa Rica, 1982.

Catão, F. *O que é teologia da libertação*. São Paulo, 1985.

Comblin, José. *O tempo da ação*. Petrópolis: Vozes, 1982.

Dussel, Enrique. *Caminhos de libertação latino-americana*. São Paulo, 1985.

————. *Historia de la Iglesia en América Latina*. Barcelona: Nova Terra, 1972. (Engl. trans., *A History of the Church in Latin America*. Grand Rapids: Eerdmans, 1981.)

Echegaray, H. *La Práctica de Jesús*. Lima, 1980. (Engl. trans., *The Practice of Jesus*, Maryknoll, N.Y.: Orbis, 1984.)

Elizondo, Virgilio. *Galilean Journey: The Mexican-American Promise*. Maryknoll, N.Y.: Orbis, 1983.

Ferm, Deane W. *Third World Liberation Theologies: An Introductory Survey*. Maryknoll, N.Y.: Orbis, 1986.

Galilea, Segundo. *Teología de la liberación*. Santiago, 1977.

————. *Espiritualidad de liberación*. Santiago, 1974.

Gibellini, Rosino, ed. *Frontiers of Theology in Latin America*. Maryknoll, N.Y.: Orbis, 1979.

Gutiérrez, Gustavo. *Beber en su propio pozo*. Lima: CEP, 1983. (Engl. trans., *We Drink from Our Own Wells: The Spiritual Journey of a People*. Maryknoll, N.Y.: Orbis, 1984.)

————. *La Fuerza historica de los pobres*. Salamanca: Sígueme, 1980. (Engl. trans., *The Power of the Poor in History*. Maryknoll, N.Y.: Orbis, 1983.)

————. *Teología de la liberación. Perspectivas*. Lima: CEP, 1971. (Engl. trans., *A Theology of Liberation*. Maryknoll, N.Y.: Orbis/London, S.C.M. Press, 1973.)

Hoornaert, E. *Historia da Igreja no Brasil*. Petrópolis: Vozes, 1977.

Libânio, J. B. *Fé e política*. São Paulo, 1985.

Mesters, Carlos. *Flor sem defesa*. Petrópolis: Vozes, 1983.

Muñoz, Ronaldo. *Igreja no povo*. Petrópolis: Vozes, 1985.

Oliveros, Roberto. *Liberación y teología*. Lima: CEP, 1977.

Pixley, George, and Boff, Clodovis. *Opção pelos pobres.* Petrópolis: Vozes, 1985.

Richard, Pablo. *Mort des Chrétientés et naissance de l'Eglise.* Paris: Centre Lebret, 1978. (Engl. trans., *Death of Christendoms and Birth of the Church.* Maryknoll, N.Y.: Orbis, 1987.)

Rubio, A. G. *Teologia da Libertação.* São Paulo, 1977.

Scannone, J. C. *Teología de la liberación y praxis popular.* Salamanca, 1976.

Segundo, J. L. *El hombre de hoy ante Jesús de Nazareth.* Madrid, 1982, 3 vols. (Engl. trans., *Jesus of Nazareth Yesterday and Today.* Maryknoll, N.Y.: Orbis, 1984–88, 5 vols.)

——. *Liberación de la teología.* Buenos Aires, 1975. (Engl. trans., *The Liberation of Theology.* Maryknoll, N.Y.: Orbis, 1976.)

Sobrino, Jon. *Cristología desde América Latina.* Mexico City, 1976. (Engl. trans., *Christology at the Crossroads.* Maryknoll, N.Y.: Orbis, 1978.)

——. *Resurrección de la verdadera Iglesia.* Santander, 1981.

Tamez, Elsa. *La Biblia de los oprimidos.* San José, Costa Rica: DEI, 1979. (Engl. trans., *Bible of the Oppressed.* Maryknoll, N.Y.: Orbis, 1982.)

Torres, Sergio. *A Igreja a partir da base.* São Paulo, 1982.